HEALTH AND WELLBEING

EXPLORE PSE

CfE Student Book

Series Editor:
Catherine Kirk

Pauline Stirling
Stephen De Silva
Lesley de Meza
Ian Geddes
Calum Campbell

HODDER
GIBSON
AN HACHETTE UK COMPANY

Every effort has been made to trace all copyright holders, but if any have been inadvertently overlooked, the Publishers will be pleased to make the necessary arrangements at the first opportunity.

Although every effort has been made to ensure that website addresses are correct at time of going to press, Hodder Education cannot be held responsible for the content of any website mentioned in this book. It is sometimes possible to find a relocated web page by typing in the address of the home page for a website in the URL window of your browser.

Hachette UK's policy is to use papers that are natural, renewable and recyclable products and made from wood grown in well-managed forests and other controlled sources. The logging and manufacturing processes are expected to conform to the environmental regulations of the country of origin.

Orders: please contact Hachette UK Distribution, Hely Hutchinson Centre, Milton Road, Didcot, Oxfordshire, OX11 7HH. Telephone: +44 (0)1235 827827. Email education@hachette.co.uk. Lines are open from 9 a.m. to 5 p.m., Monday to Friday. You can also order through our website: www.hoddereducation.co.uk

ISBN: 978 1 3983 1186 2

© Calum Campbell, Ian Geddes, Pauline Stirling, Stephen De Silva and Lesley de Meza 2021

First published in 2021 by

Hodder Gibson, an imprint of Hodder Education,

An Hachette UK Company

211 St Vincent Street

Glasgow G2 5QY

www.hoddergibson.co.uk

Impression number 10 9 8 7 6 5 4 3 2 1

Year   2025 2024 2023 2022 2021

Cover photo © rizal999 – stock.adobe.com; © melosine1302 – stock.adobe.com; © Richard Wendt

Illustrations by Aptara Inc.

Typeset in Frutiger LTStd-Light 11/13 pts. by Aptara Inc.

Printed in India

A catalogue record for this title is available from the British Library.

Contents

Contents

Getting the most from this book

Welcome to the *Explore PSE for CfE Student Book*. This book is designed to help young people grow and develop as individuals, and provide a wide ranging Personal and Social Education course that is mapped to the guidelines provided by the Scottish Government, SQA, and Education Scotland.

The course takes an active learning approach, which means that you, the student, will be invited to participate and contribute to the learning opportunities in a variety of different ways.

In terms of how this book is structured, each chapter of is made up of a series of learning opportunities. The chapters and learning opportunities are all numbered, but your teacher may decide to deliver these in another order, catered more specifically to the individual needs and aims of your school. You should also be aware that there may be other local examples or sources available that will give you additional resources and add to your information and understanding.

The following features have been included to help you get the most from this book:

Learning outcomes

Learning outcomes highlight what you will have learned by the end of each learning opportunity, and help you track progress throughout the course.

Starter

Starters include a short activity to help introduce you to each topic and get you thinking.

Activity

Activities throughout the book will ask you to engage with the material in many different ways, from group activities to word sorts.

Sources, ranging from illustrations and photos to newspaper extracts and information from websites will provide the basis for activities, and stimulate discussion within the class.

What am I going to learn in PSE?

Let's find out!

✓ learning with each other

✓ learning from each other

✓ bringing your own ideas and thoughts

✓ sharing them together

✓ listening to each other

✓ finding out what you have in common

✓ thinking about what is important to you.

Source 1 What is PSE all about?

Acknowledgements

Hodder Education would like to thank the following organisations for their invaluable input and reviews:

Chapter 2 Growing up, Chapter 3 Relationships, and Chapter 4 Sex, sexuality and sexual health were kindly reviewed by Brook. Brook is a sexual health and wellbeing charity, and has been at the forefront of providing wellbeing and sexual health support for young people for over 50 years. For more information, you can visit: www.brook.org.uk.

Chapter 5 Alcohol, tobacco and other drugs was kindly reviewed by Drugs and Me. Drugs and Me is an educational website providing freely accessible, unbiased, and non-judgemental harm reduction information for alcohol, tobacco and other recreational drugs. You can find out more at: www.drugsand.me.

Chapter 8, learning opportunity 8.7 Female genital mutilation (FGM) was kindly reviewed by FORWARD (Foundation for Women's Health Research and Development), an African women-led organisation working to end violence against women and girls. For more information, you can visit: www.forwarduk.org.uk.

By the end of 1.1 you will:
- be able to say what PSE education is all about
- be able to identify which skills and qualities are important in PSE learning opportunities.

Starter

Think back to when you were in Primary 7. What did you enjoy, what were you looking forward to, and what did you worry about?

In small groups, divide a large piece of paper into four sections with the headings:

1 We were worried about …
2 Outside school we enjoyed …
3 In school we enjoyed …
4 We were looking forward to …

Then fill in the sections with your ideas. Agree and feed back on the most important thing for each section.

Activity 1

In pairs, look at the photos in Source 1. What personal development might be happening in each of the situations?

The starter activity is what PSE will be about: learning with each other and from each other. All of us learn and develop at school and in our wider lives outside school. We learn at school, at home, when out and about, at the sports centre – we may not realise it but we are learning all the time. This is part of what we call 'personal development'.

PERSONAL DEVELOPMENT = Life + The Universe + Everything

Source 1 Wherever we go, whoever we talk to, we are always learning

PSE learning opportunities are just one place where we can think about things that are important to each of us, and how we live in the wider world.

The letters PSE stand for:

Personal
and
Social
Education

Activity 2

In this PSE book, we will be looking at several areas that will affect your development personally and socially. Source 2 below includes some of the topics you will be learning about in PSE. These topics can be divided into the headings 'Personal', 'Social', 'Health' and 'Financial'. In groups, organise the words under the these headings (Personal, Social, Health and Financial). This might require a 'best fit' approach! In your groups brainstorm some other topics you think might be covered under each of the headings.

Me and my family	Eating well	Saving pocket money	Feelings
Making choices	Keeping safe	Looking ahead	The wider world
Not smoking	Exercise	Working with others	Friends	Good communication

Source 2 Topics you will learn about

Activity 3

Think back over how you have worked with others in this learning opportunity. On your own, read and reflect on the checklist on the right. Which of these skills did you use? How do you know you used these skills well? How important are these skills going to be in PSE learning opportunities? How can you develop skills and qualities to ensure you can work with others in a safe and positive way? Are there other skills and attributes that will be important in PSE learning opportunities?

Be prepared to feed back on your thoughts to the class.

✓ learning with each other

✓ learning from each other

✓ bringing your own ideas and thoughts

✓ sharing ideas and thoughts together

✓ listening to each other

✓ finding out what you have in common

✓ thinking about what is important to you.

By the end of 1.2 you will:
- be able to describe what the values of PSE are
- have produced a Group Agreement to maintain a safe, positive working environment.

We all have ideas by which we live, for example, 'it is important to help other people', 'we should treat other people the same way we would like to be treated', and so on. Sometimes we call these ideas 'values'.

Your PSE course gives you the opportunity to consider your own and others' values – Source 1, the rainbow diagram, is an example of this.

Source 1 PSE values

Starter

In pairs, look at the rainbow of PSE values in Source 1 and identify something that everyone could do to work within these values.

The values in Source 1 are one way of describing how you can work with each other in PSE learning opportunities. We can use these to develop a Group Agreement which will outline the rights and responsibilities you share.

In PSE each of us has the right to …

Be heard.

So each person also has the responsibility to …

Listen to others when they speak.

In PSE each of us has the right to …

So each person also has the responsibility to …

In PSE each of us has the right to …

So each person also has the responsibility to …

Source 2 An example of a Group Agreement

Young people in Scotland were asked by the Scottish Government to come up with a Charter setting out how they would like to be treated. The Charter in Source 3 on the right is what they came up with.

Activity 1

Work together in small groups to come up with a Group Agreement. It should outline the rights and responsibilities you think you should share in PSE. Use the example in Source 2 to help you.

A Charter for Young People

Get to know us

Speak with us

Listen to us

Take us seriously

Involve us

Respect our privacy

Be responsible to us

Think about our lives as a whole

Think carefully about how you use information about us

Put us in touch with the right people

Use your power to help

Make things happen when they should

Help us be safe

Source 3 Protecting Children and Young People: The Charter

Activity 2

Now that each small group has agreed its own Group Agreement. Now is the time for each group to feed these ideas back to the class to come up with a Group Agreement for the whole class.

The Group Agreement has been set. In pairs, consider:
* How can you make sure everyone in the class remembers the terms of the Group Agreement?
* How can you encourage everyone in the class to abide by the Group Agreement?
* How will you know that the Group Agreement is being kept to?
* How can you judge the effectiveness of the Group Agreement?
* What can you do if you feel the Group Agreement is not working?

Be prepared to feed your thoughts back to the class.

Activity 3

Can you think of examples of Group Agreements in everyday life? For example, the Highway Code is a Group Agreement which has become law. A more informal example is the acceptance of speaking quietly and only when necessary in a library, allowing others to concentrate.

Activity 4

On your own, read and reflect on the Charter in Source 3. If you were given the opportunity to ask adults to listen to you, what would you include in your Charter?

By the end of 2.1 you will:

- be able to describe the changes you are experiencing as a secondary school student
- be able to identify ways to support yourself and other students who are new to the school.

Starter

You might have attended an induction/transition/bump-up day before you came to your new school for First Year (S1) or moved up to your secondary school stage. On this day there was a lot to take in. You may not have wanted to ask questions. What most worried you about coming to your new school? In pairs, reflect upon the ways in which your new school is different from your primary school. In Source 1 you can see some ideas from students your age about how to make the change to a new school, or step up to First Year (S1), as smooth as possible. Discuss these with your partner and agree on which three you think are the most important.

Throughout the rest of this learning opportunity you will think about ways to support yourself and other students who are new to the school.

Have confidence. Don't worry or be scared.

Be prepared/organised – make sure you have the right equipment.

If someone is causing trouble or upsetting another person, don't join in.

Make new friends but don't forget your old ones.

Take advice from teachers and good friends.

Don't be afraid – reporting bullying (towards you or other people) is a good thing.

Get your homework in on time.

Listen to your teachers and do as you are told the first time.

Be a good person – kind, nice, friendly and polite towards others.

Ask for help if you need it.

Source 1 'A new school survival guide'

Activity 1

It's good to have a personal checklist to help you keep organised and happy at school. What kind of things would you put on your list?

Complete this sentence: 'My top tip to myself to be successful at my new school is …'

Activity 2

Imagine you had to write a guide to the school for First Year (S1). What does a First Year (S1) student need to know? What would be useful? Look at the examples in Source 2 to give you some ideas.

As a class decide on the headings for the guide. Work together in small groups. Each group plans and writes one section of the guide. Share your section of the guide with the rest of the class.

Moving around between classrooms

Names of teachers

What extra-curricular activities there are

House/tutor and/or year group systems

Making new friends

Where and when assemblies are held

The layout of the school and classrooms

Who to speak to if things go wrong

Source 2 Settling in at school

How the canteen works

Activity 3

On your own, think about what you found most useful in helping you to settle in at this school. Be prepared to feed back to the class.

By the end of 2.2 you will:
- be able to describe the physical and emotional changes of puberty
- identify ways to manage these changes appropriately.

Starter

When it comes to the word 'puberty', people may be embarrassed as we talk about the private parts of the body. People might use slang names to describe these parts. It's important to know the scientific names for the reproductive organs and sexual parts (see list below). But let's start by sharing slang names that you know!

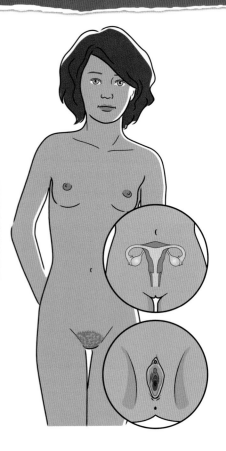

Female bodies

Clitoris – the visible part of this organ is above the urethra, but most of this large organ is internal, sometimes reaching more than five inches around the labia. It contains thousands of nerve endings and gives pleasurable feelings when touched.

Fallopian tube(s) – the egg passes down this towards the uterus.

Ovaries – where eggs are produced.

Urethra – the opening that urine (wee) comes out of.

Uterus/Womb – where a baby grows from a fertilised egg. When an egg is not fertilised, the special lining of the womb is shed each month. This is called 'having a period' (menstruation) and happens from puberty onwards.

Vagina – the opening passage through which menstrual blood passes, in which sexual intercourse can take place and through which a baby could be born.

Vulva – the area between the legs which is made up of the outer and inner labia, the opening to the urethra, the clitoris and the opening to the vagina.

Male bodies

Foreskin – a layer of skin covering the end of the penis. The top part of the foreskin can be removed for health or religious reasons (circumcision).

Penis – the organ that hangs in front of the scrotum, the urethra is a tube through the middle of the penis.

Scrotum – a sack of soft skin that covers and protects the two testicles.

Testicles – in the scrotum and often called 'balls'. They make sperm, which can fertilise eggs to make a baby.

Urethra – the narrow tube inside the penis that carries sperm and urine out of the body.

And finally, remember that all genitalia come in all different shapes and sizes.

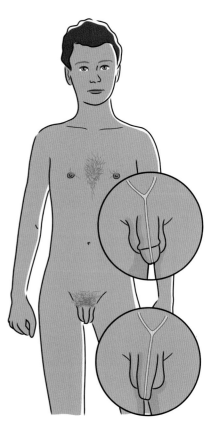

Source 1 Female and male bodies

Right now you are probably in a class with people who are around the same age as you. If you look around, you will notice that some people are tall, and others are shorter. Some people have big feet and others have small feet. The fact is that puberty happens at different rates and not at exactly the same time for each person. It is natural to worry about feeling different – that you aren't like everyone else seems to be, but at some point everyone will catch up and reach their own adult size.

Puberty is the process of physical and emotional changes through which a child's body matures into an adult body capable of sexual reproduction. It is initiated by hormonal signals from the brain to the ovaries in a female body, preparing for menstruation, and the testes in a male body. The young person may have sexual feelings that they have never felt before.

It is important to remember that every body is different. So it makes sense that genitalia, that is the penis, testicles, vagina, vulva, also come in different shapes and sizes. Additionally, what is shown in the media is not always a reflection of what is normal.

Maja is twelve. She really enjoys PE, especially athletics, and always looks forward to the learning opportunity. However, she has noticed recently that, at around the same time each month, her breasts are sore when she runs and she is worried that this is slowing her down.

Lou and Max are both at the same school and they have a lot of learning opportunities together. Lou thinks about Max all the time and is having trouble concentrating in learning opportunities.

Anthony finds that he gets erections quite randomly. It's not so bad when he is in his school uniform as he is sure that nobody notices, but he worries that it will happen in PE when he is wearing his PE kit and that people will notice.

Source 2 Changes

Activity 1

Some of the words you identified in the Starter activity may cause offence to some people. One way to make sure that no one gets upset and that we all understand each other is to agree which words to use. Copy the diagram of the male and female bodies in Source 1. See how many of the parts of the diagram you can label, using the words in bold. Compare your answers with a partner.

Activity 2

Read scenarios in Source 2 about young people who have begun the journey through puberty. Discuss what changes they might be experiencing. Use the following three headings to help you think about this:
- Physical – How are their bodies changing?
- Emotional – How are their feelings changing?
- Social – How are their relationships with family and friends changing?

What other changes can be experienced during puberty? Add to your list. Is there any advice you could give to enable these young people to cope well with what they are going through?

Activity 3

Think back over all the things you've talked about in this learning opportunity. You may still have questions that you would like answered. On a slip of paper write down one question that you would like to ask privately, fold it up and give it to your teacher. You need to remember to write your name on the slip of paper. Your teacher will try to answer your question or will help you to find the answer.

Remember that although your teacher won't share what you have written unless necessary, they cannot promise to keep to themselves anything that puts you or anyone at risk.

Menstrual wellbeing

By the end of 2.3 you will:
- understand the changes that occur with menstruation
- be able to identify ways to manage menstruation.

Starter

What do you know about periods? Work with a partner to make a list of all the things you know. Be prepared to share your ideas.

What do you need to know?

- Menstruation, or having a period, is when blood is discharged through the vagina. The lining of the uterus builds up every month to prepare female bodies to feed and grow a baby if an egg is fertilised. If a baby is not conceived, the lining is not needed and this leads to menstruation.
- Menstruation can begin as early as eight years old or as late as 18.
- Periods take place around once a month, although this can vary.
- The bleeding usually continues for approximately 4-7 days, although again, this can vary.
- Some people experience heavy periods while others have very light ones. This is a normal part of life and does not stop them from carrying out their everyday activities.
- It's useful to be prepared by having supplies in a bag or locker and making a note on a calendar on the first day of a period to keep track. There are also apps that help to track periods. However, when someone first starts to have periods, they may not experience regular monthly bleeding. It can take up to two years for periods to become regular. This can be challenging as hygiene and coping skills may have to be relearned once again after a few months. Just like any new skill, practice and patience are required.
- It is vital to wash hands both before and after changing a pad, tampon or menstrual cup. Tampons and pads need to be properly disposed of (they must never be flushed down the toilet).
- Even when someone has been having periods for a while, the cycle may be the same every month or it may change. Stress, sickness, medical conditions and medications can all change the number of days. However, if someone does not have a period and is having sex, they may be pregnant. In that case, they must ask for medical advice.
- Period pain is common and a normal part of the menstrual cycle. It's usually felt as muscle cramps. The pain sometimes comes in intense spasms, while at other times it may be dull but more constant. It may also vary with each period.
- Pre-menstrual syndrome (PMS) can occur any time in the two weeks before menstruation. It can make someone feel moody, irritable, have tender breasts or bloating.

Activity 1

How many of you have seen adverts on TV about pads or tampons? What products are available? Look at Source 1.

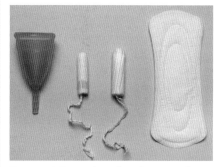

Source 1 Examples of sanitary products

What products are available?

Pads are special cotton filled, plastic lined pads used to collect menstrual blood. They come in different sizes for the different flows. Also, some pads come with wings that wrap around the leg openings of underwear. Most have a sticky strip that holds the pad to underwear. Pads should be changed often. You can also get reusable pads, and pants made of fabric that are washed and re-used rather than disposed of, and are therefore more environmentally friendly.

Panty liners are similar to pads. They are used to collect light menstrual flow or vaginal discharge.

Tampons are another way to collect menstrual blood. Some people like to use tampons as they keep the blood inside the vagina. They are made of soft cotton and have a string attached to the bottom. Tampons are inserted into the vagina with the string hanging down through the vaginal opening. Some tampons have a cardboard tube to help them to be inserted. The tampon is removed by pulling gently on the string. Tampons need to be changed often (at least every 3–4 hours).

Inserting a tampon for the first time can be tricky. There are usually instructions in the tampon box about how to put them into the vagina. It helps to remember that the vagina slopes backwards. Before using tampons it is important to read the leaflet contained in the packet, this contains safety information.

Menstrual cups are reusable cups made of silicone which can be inserted into the vagina. They form a plug in the vagina catching the blood. A person would need more than one. They should be removed regularly and washed, and then reinserted, during your period.

There are now **period clothing items** available, for example, leggings, which can be worn to provide extra protection during a period. There is also underwear which can be worn instead of pads, liners, tampons or cups, or can be worn as additional protection.

If you have started your period, you …	Yes	No
Should wash your hands before and after changing a pad, tampon or cup		
Should flush your pad down the toilet		
Should always have a pad, tampon or cup with you		
Have your period every four weeks		
Might have a stronger vaginal discharge that smells strong or unpleasant (and this is normal)		
Cannot play sports		
Can expect each period to always last a week		
Need to change your tampon, pad or cup regularly		
Cannot use tampons until you've been menstruating for at least a year		

Activity 2

In pairs, answer these questions.
1 Does someone who has started their periods always need to carry sanitary pads or tampons with them?
2 What could someone do if they start their period at school and don't have a pad or a tampon with them?
3 How can they ask for one? Who could they ask?

Activity 3

What advice can you give these people?

Cam is in a History exam in the hall and thinks she feels that her period has started.

Katelyn is going camping with school at the weekend. She looks on the calendar and sees that her period is due.

Mhairi has PE next. Her period is due but she realises she has no sanitary products with her in school.

Activity 4

In pairs, answer yes or no to the statements on the left. Be prepared to feed back to the class.

Activity 5

Growing up and changing can be exciting and scary at the same time. If you have any worries or concerns about any of the physical or emotional changes of puberty, who can you speak to?

By the end of 2.4 you will:

- understand the importance of personal hygiene
- be able to identify ways of achieving and maintaining healthy hygiene practices.

Starter

In pairs, make a list of all the things that you can think of that people do every day to look after their own personal hygiene. For example: wash hands, brush teeth, use deodorant …

Be prepared to feed back to the class.

Personal hygiene means making sure the visible parts of the body are kept clean. Not keeping up standards of personal hygiene leads to an increased risk of infection or illness, as well as having social implications.

While personal hygiene helps you to keep looking and feeling fresh, it also helps to prevent sickness, infection, and embarrassment.

Activity 1

In pairs, use the table to think about which parts of the body in particular we need to keep clean. Consider how and what would happen if we don't do this. Are there any social implications related to body odour, bad teeth or smelly feet? What effect might it have on others if you did not wash your hands properly after using the toilet? Do we need to buy any special products?

What needs our attention?	How do we keep it/ them clean?	What product/s can we use to help?	Physical effects if we don't do this	Negative social effects
Teeth	Brush twice a day Floss regularly Visit the dentist regularly	Toothpaste Dental floss Mouthwash	Toothache Tooth decay Bad breath Loss of teeth	Bad breath is unpleasant for others Poor appearance Friends?
Hands				
Hair				
Skin on face				
Skin on body				
Armpits (including hair)				
Feet				
Runny nose				
Groin area				

Lani, twelve, is a keen football player, and spends most of her free time practising her field skills. Ever since she hit puberty, she has noticed a foul smell when she sweats during practice. She is embarrassed as she is sure that others will have noticed too. She talks to her friend about what is troubling her. Her friend explains that he had the same problem and had plucked up the courage to ask his dad for advice. His dad explained that during puberty, different glands in the armpits and groin area are triggered and release chemicals that cause a bad smell. His dad told him how to control the sweating and smells, advising him to shower regularly and to use an antiperspirant or deodorant.

Lani keeps up with her body's needs and also makes sure she changes her football kit and underwear daily. She is often tired (puberty does that) and she has a busy life outside school. She has more homework than when in primary school and has to travel further to get to school, so she really does need to make time to keep clean and fresh but she knows it is worth it.

Activity 2

If you manage your personal hygiene properly, there is nothing to be embarrassed about. You need to make time to manage your personal hygiene. In pairs, write a short poem similar to the ones in Source 1, to encourage young people to think about their personal hygiene.

During puberty, sweat glands in the groin, armpits and on our feet become more active, producing more sweat. Fresh sweat doesn't smell but if it is left to build up on skin or clothing, bacteria on our skin act on it and cause the characteristic body odour smell. (Body odour is often called BO.) You learned in primary school that you need to wash your hands after using the toilet and that you need to clean your teeth twice a day, but now this is even more important than ever.

Puberty is also a good time to start using antiperspirant deodorant. Note that there are many products that are *deodorants* but not all are *antiperspirants*. Deodorant products simply cover up smells whereas antiperspirants stop body odour by controlling how much you sweat.

Although all young people have the same basic hygiene issues, you might also begin to think about shaving (how to do it and when to start) or when you menstruate. You also need to consider how often to change a pad, cup or tampon, and how to dispose of pads and tampons hygienically.

Wash your hands
Before you eat
Change socks daily
Look after your feet.

Brush your teeth
Twice a day
Shower regularly
Keep odours at bay.

Activity 3

Share your poem with the class. Choose the best ones to make a class personal hygiene pledge. Have you covered everything? Have you thought about products that you might use? Remember that personal hygiene is important and not something to be embarrassed about.

Source 1 Two poems about personal hygiene

By the end of 2.5 you will:
- understand how feelings change as we grow and mature
- be able to identify ways to build confidence to be able to cope with these changes.

Starter

1   Can you remember how you felt on the very first day at this school? Were you nervous, excited, worried? Did you know anybody else coming to this school?
2   Compared with then, how have your feelings changed? Why might you feel more relaxed about your school now?

Coping with change is something that we have to do throughout life. Puberty is a time that brings lots of changes. Puberty is the term that describes the changes that take you on a journey from being a child to becoming an adult: it is a time of many changes. These changes include things that happen to our bodies, as well as our emotions and our relationships with other people. The hormones that make all the physical changes happen also affect our feelings and emotions. We just can't see them!

People are at different places on the journey – some are happy not being too grown-up and others can't wait to be adults. Some are even-tempered while others find their moods change quickly – one minute they're feeling really happy to go along with friends and the next they don't want to talk to anyone!

Activity 1

Look at the words in Source 1. They describe some of the emotions that young people feel as they go through all the changes of puberty. Not everyone finds it easy to talk about these emotions.

Which two of these emotions might come up most often in young people's conversations? Why did you choose those two emotions? Imagine you could tell advisers on a young people's helpline how to prepare to talk to young people. What would you say?

embarrassed   worried   sad   bothered   just OK   different
confused   stupid   bored   amazed   interested   fantastic
nervous   inquisitive   annoyed   scared   curious   angry
baffled   lonely

Source 1

I've got massive spots all over my face. Feel like everyone's looking at me and thinking I'm ugly – just want to hide.

All my friends are talking about getting off with people – no one would ever fancy me.

All my friends get to stay out late at weekends but my parents won't let me. What's wrong with them, it's not like I have school the next day?! They treat me like a child!

Everything's gone wrong for me. I keep falling out with my friends over silly things and now my best mate has started hanging around with new people and doesn't really speak to me anymore. I just feel like crying all the time.

I really fancy this boy in the year above but I don't think he knows I even exist. I dream about him all the time. I was thinking about sending him a message.

Source 2 Messages

Activity 2

Look at Source 2 which shows messages from young people of about your age. They all feel that they're facing problems that are part of changing and growing up. Work with a friend to reply to these messages. Imagine that it is your job to give advice, reassurance and sources of help.

Activity 3

Imagine that local secondary schools are contributing to teenagers' blog pages of a youth website. Your school is focusing on the topic of 'Puberty and growing up'. You will need to think about how puberty might affect someone's emotions and what might help. In small groups, you can focus on one topic area and come up with a heading for your topic. This could be something like how to negotiate with your family and could be called: 'Why do my family act this way?' Or it could be signposting who to talk to or where to seek help and be called: 'Who to talk to?'

One way of helping people who feel distressed is to give them confidence to do things they will enjoy so you could think of ideas for blog pieces to encourage young people to explore new interests. You might also want to think of people who could be interviewed – especially local people who already work in ways that help and support young people. You and your team need to produce plans for the sort of blog pieces the website would feature for young secondary school students.

By the end of 2.6 you will:
- understand that relationships affect everything we do
- understand that positive friendships are important in our lives
- understand that friendships can cause strong feelings and emotions.

Starter

What does it mean to be a good friend?
In pairs, answer this question. Be prepared to feed back to the class.

You are either at or you are approaching the age when you may choose to sign up to a social networking site. We can reduce some of the risks online by making sure we have good privacy settings. We need to be careful about the information we give online. We also need to remember that people we meet online might not be exactly who they say they are.

Activity 1

Imagine that you are going to create a friendship profile for a social media site.

Look at Source 1 and use it to give you some ideas for how to create your profile. Think carefully about the images and phrases you will use to get your message across. Think about your personal characteristics – what are your interests and hobbies, what qualities have you got that make you a great friend?

Friend available

My name is Frankie, I'm thirteen and I'm the best friend you could ever hope to have! I like music – both listening to it and performing! I play the drums and I have lessons after school. I am a good listener and am very patient (I have two younger sisters so I have to be!). I was nervous about coming to a new school but I needn't have been as everyone is friendly.

Source 1 Friend available

Activity 2

Even the best of friends find that they sometimes disagree or even fall out with each other. Do you think having arguments is a natural part of being friends? What sorts of things do friends argue about? Come up with a list of things that might cause an argument between friends.

Activity 3

Read Source 2, a list of situations in which friends might fall out or disagree. Work together with someone and come up with simple suggestions for solving the problem. What would you have to do, and what would your friend have to do, to keep the friendship going?

You were invited to spend the night at a friend's house. Half an hour before you were due to leave, your friend texts to cancel. The next day you find out that someone else was invited instead of you.

You and your friend have decided to join an after-school club. There are two activities that you both want to take part in; however, they are both scheduled at the same time.

For the last couple of months you have been going round to your best friend's house every day after school. You enjoy it but are beginning to feel you'd like to do other things too.

You and your friend have done something wrong and now your parents or carers have found out. You tell the truth but your friend lies and doesn't admit to being involved.

You've lent a favourite item of clothing to a friend and they return it dirty and with a hole in it.

Source 2 Friendship conflicts

Activity 4

Look at the notes in Source 3 that have been started for you and, on your own, decide on one thing you would put under each heading.

The number one friendship skill is … *being a good listener.*

The one thing I look for in a friend is … *honesty.*

The best thing I can offer another friend is … *my loyalty.*

Note:

More information about online safety and how to report concerns can be found at **www.thinkuknow.co.uk**.

Source 3 Notes on friendship

By the end of 3.1 you will:
- be able to name different types of relationships
- be able to identify some of the qualities needed to maintain good relationships
- understand that most relationships go through positive and negative phases, and need to be maintained.

Starter

What is a relationship?

In pairs, discuss who you have spoken to, or interacted with in some way, today. What is the relationship you have with that person?

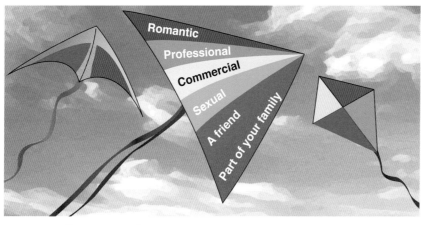

Source 1 Different types of relationships

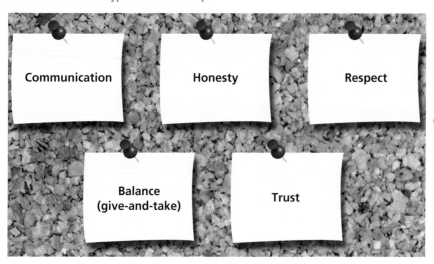

Source 2 Five qualities

Activity 1

Look at Source 1. Which type of relationship do the following people belong to? Some people could belong to more than one type.
- a girl/boyfriend
- b step-parent
- c shop assistant
- d teacher
- e aunt/uncle
- f doctor (GP)
- g neighbour of your age
- h bus driver
- i person with shared interest, e.g. online gamer
- j life partner, husband, wife
- k carer/foster carer

Activity 2

Look at Source 2 and the five qualities. Which of these do you think is the most important in maintaining a good relationship?

In any kind of relationship there are qualities that will make the relationship work better for the people involved. For example:

- communication – listening to each other and clearly expressing yourself

- honesty – speaking openly about what is going well or not so well in your relationship.

Activity 3

Look at Source 3. What might be the positive and negative experiences of the people in these relationships?

Going out with your best friend's 'ex'

Being in an arranged relationship/marriage

Living together with step-siblings (step-brothers/sisters)

Having your parent's new partner in the house

Source 3 Examples of types of relationships

Activity 4

This topic has been about different types of relationships and how we try to maintain good relationships. Every relationship will experience its up and downs – life isn't always about having the perfect family and friends, and living happily ever after.

Think about one relationship that you have in your life. What qualities do you have that can keep that relationship healthy?

By the end of 3.2 you will:

- be able to say what makes a healthy relationship
- be able to identify the warning signs of an unhealthy relationship.

Starter

Think about the many different relationships which you have with people. Now consider how each of these people makes you feel. In pairs, discuss what is needed to make a relationship healthy. Be prepared to feed back to the class.

Mutual respect

If you have respect for someone then you value that person. Mutual respect in a relationship means valuing each other. It means understanding, and not challenging, each other's boundaries.

Trust

Trust is very important in a relationship. It is about trusting and being trustworthy. It is difficult to respect someone that you don't trust.

Honesty

It is not easy to trust someone who is dishonest. Honesty and trust go together. Honesty is also about speaking openly and sharing feelings. So honesty is also linked to good communication.

Communication

Good communication is all about being able to express yourself clearly and about listening well to others.

Fairness/equality

Being fair is about give and take, sometimes about compromising. It's about having an equal relationship. It's about mutual respect and reciprocity.

Source 1 Key concepts of a healthy relationship

What's an unhealthy relationship?

You will notice that the key concepts in Source 1 are inter-linked and overlap. If you remove one key concept from a relationship, it affects other key concepts. For example, if someone is dishonest then it is difficult to trust them … without trust, it is unlikely there would be mutual respect … a lack of mutual respect might make the relationship unequal and unfair … dishonesty might mean keeping secrets and so not being open and not communicating well … and so on.

So what does an unhealthy relationship look like?

Can you think of any examples of unhealthy relationships or unhealthy behaviours in relationships shown by celebrities?

Activity 1

Source 1 shows key concepts in a healthy relationship. In pairs, read each concept and think of an example that would support this. For example, when you and a friend go to the cinema and you discuss what you want to watch beforehand, and come to an agreement, this is fair. And the fairness shows respect for one another.

A healthy relationship can be contrasted with an unhealthy relationship – an unequal relationship does not have mutuality, respect and reciprocity. It is where one person has more power or control and manipulates or takes advantage of the other person.

Activity 2

In pairs, read the scenarios in Source 2 and discuss the positive and negative elements within the relationships. Look at the key concepts needed to make a relationship healthy (Source 1) and decide whether they are present. Check the warning signs of an unhealthy relationship in Source 3. Decide, on balance, whether the relationship is healthy or unhealthy.

Be prepared to explain your decision when feeding back to the class.

Scenario 1

Karl and Michael have been friends since primary school. They live in the same village and get the school bus together into town. They are both now in secondary school but, unfortunately, they have very few learning opportunities together this year. Both have made new friends in their new classes and Karl has joined football after school one night a week with his new friends. However, they really enjoy catching up on the bus journey when they chat about their experiences in the new school and laugh about things that have happened in learning opportunities! They still meet up at least once at the weekend.

Scenario 2

Jordan and Cam have been 'a couple' since the start of term. It really was 'love at first sight' when Cam joined the school. Cam has recently moved to the area and so knew nobody at school at the start of term, whereas Jordan had a big friendship group. Jordan has always enjoyed playing drums in the school band. Cam doesn't like Jordan's friends and gets annoyed when Jordan wants to see them. Jordan has agreed to give up band to spend more time with Cam, but Cam thinks Jordan might be secretly attending practices. Recently, Jordan has noticed that Cam is always waiting outside the classroom at the start of lunch and the end of the day.

Scenario 3

Charley tries hard to please Nic but it is not easy. Nic is often in a bad mood when they are together. Nic always criticises how Charley dresses but when Charley wears something new, Nic criticises that too! Charley would love to hear Nic say 'You look nice today!' Charley would do anything to please Nic and has tried everything from a new hairstyle to a fake tan! But Charley is never good enough for Nic.

Scenario 4

Michele is 12 and Kiera is 14. They are sisters and they share a bedroom in their three-bedroom home. They have a little brother, Dylan, who is 8. He is lucky enough to have his own room. Michele likes to read, enjoys her own company and prefers peace and quiet. Kiera, on the other hand, likes to listen to music – and the louder the better! So, the girls have talked it through and come to an agreement: if they are both in the bedroom, then it is quiet; but Michele goes downstairs to read sometimes so that Kiera can play her music. It works!

Scenario 5

Jamie and Stevie have been chatting online. Jamie thinks Stevie is 16 like Jamie is, but in fact Stevie is only 13. Stevie never lied when they first met online, but Jamie just assumed that Stevie was 16 and Stevie went along with it. It is now becoming obvious that Jamie is looking for more in the relationship. Jamie wants to meet up with Stevie and has suggested that they meet in town one evening.

Scenario 6

Kim has become very dependent on Jaz. They have known each other since they were in nursery school and have always gone everywhere together. Jaz now wants to spend time with new friends but is worried about letting Kim down. Jaz feels that perhaps a clean break is best, but worries how it will make Kim feel.

Source 2 Relationship scenarios

Warning signs of an unhealthy relationship

What if they…

- expect to get their own way and then get angry if they don't?
- don't let me see my friends?
- put me down in front of other people?
- make me feel that I am not good enough?
- say that nobody else would want to be my friend or go out with me?
- dictate what I do in my free time?
- have ever gone to hit me?
- tried to make me do something that I am not comfortable with?

Source 3 The warning signs of an unhealthy relationship

Activity 3

Think about what you have learnt today. Choose one relationship that you have which you would consider healthy. What are the key concepts that make that relationship healthy? What is that relationship built on? Trust? Honesty? Respect?

Be prepared to feed back to the class.

By the end of 3.3 you will:
- know how to express yourself clearly, share feelings openly and listen to others
- be able to explain what 'assertiveness' is.

Starter

Work with a partner. Decide who is A and who is B. Take a piece of paper each and a pencil, and sit back-to-back. Partner A draws a simple picture and then describes it for B so that they can draw the same. Compare the pictures. How similar are they? How easy was this activity for A and for B? What were the difficulties, if any? Then swap over and do the same again, this time with B drawing first and describing the picture to A.

Both times, you had to rely solely on good clear verbal expression and good listening skills. Was it easier the second time and if so, why? It may have been easier the second time because you had already experienced what it is like to communicate only verbally – so without any hand gestures.

Activity 1

Write a paragraph about something that you did at the weekend or during the holidays. Work with a partner. Take it in turns to read your paragraphs to each other.

Reader: Make sure that you express yourself clearly.

Listener: Listen carefully and don't be afraid to ask questions if you don't understand.

Good communication skills guide

1 Listening

One of the best ways to be a good communicator is to be a good listener. Nobody likes communicating with someone who does not take the time to listen to them. If you're not a good listener, it's going to be hard to understand what you're being asked to do.

Take the time to practise active listening. Active listening involves:

- paying close attention to what the other person is saying
- asking questions to make sure you've understood what they are saying
- rephrasing what the person says to ensure understanding ('So, what you're saying is …')

Through active listening, you can better understand what the other person is trying to say, and can respond appropriately.

2 Non-verbal communication

Your body language, eye contact, hand gestures and tone of voice all add to the message you are trying to get across. Eye contact is also important; looking the other person in the eye will show that you are focused on that person and their conversation. (Avoid staring at the person as this may make them feel uncomfortable!)

Also, be sure to notice other people's non-verbal signals while you are talking. Non-verbal signals often show how a person is really feeling. For example, if they are feeling uncomfortable or are maybe hiding the truth, they may not look you directly in the eye.

3 Clarity

Express yourself clearly and directly, and think carefully about what you are trying to say. If you talk at length, your listener may lose interest or be unsure of the point you were trying to make.

4 Confidence

It is important to be assertive and confident when you interact with others. Confidence shows that you have faith in what you're saying. Try not to make statements that sound like questions. Always try to be listening to and empathising with the other person. Of course, be careful not to sound arrogant or aggressive.

$\Rightarrow$

5 Empathy

Using simple phrases such as 'I understand what you are saying', shows that you have been listening to the other person and that you respect their opinions.

6 Respect

Show respect for the other person and their thoughts, ideas and feelings. Simple actions like using a person's name, making eye contact and actively listening when a person speaks will make the person feel appreciated.

1 Galina

Galina is 15. She has known Si, who's 16 and part of her crowd, for a couple of years. Last time they were all together Si asked her out on her own. Galina was really happy as she likes Si. At the end of the evening Si and Galina went back to Galina's

house. While they were sitting on the couch, she tried to kiss her... Galina doesn't want to fall out with her – she's known her ages – but she isn't sure she's ready for this type of relationship.

2 Hua-Ling

Hua-Ling is 14. She met Zak at the fair and they've been seeing each other for three weeks. He is quite a bit older than her and is really good looking – she's the envy of all her friends.

Hua-Ling doesn't want to tell Zak how old she is in case he thinks she is too young to be going out with.

3 Eden

Eden is 14 and is choosing which National Qualifications he will study in Fourth Year at school. He is a conscientious student who loves studying English, and is also a talented musician and a good cross-country runner. His parents

encourage him to do well. He belongs to a cross-country club and plays the trombone in a brass band. Eden takes the subject application form out of the options pack to read it and realises that his Mum had already filled it in! Mum sees the surprised look on Eden's face and says 'Well, your Dad and I discussed it and we all already know what you are going to do when you are older, don't we?'

4 Louise

Louise is 13. She lives with her dad and twin siblings Rosie and Rebecca. The house is small with two bedrooms, which means that Louise, Rosie and Rebecca share a room. Rosie is always nagging at Louise as she leaves her

clothes on the floor which makes the bedroom untidy, and Rebecca gets annoyed when Louise plays her music loud. Rosie and Rebecca are 11 and Louise feels they don't understand what it is like for her, having to share her space with two younger siblings.

Source 1 Communication skills

You need to learn good communication skills so that you can express yourself clearly, share feelings openly and listen to others. Sometimes, a problem arises in a relationship because of poor communication. Often, a problem could be solved with good communication skills.

Activity 2

With a partner, read the guide and scenarios in Source 1. How could good communication skills help Galina, Hua-Ling, Eden and Louise in each situation? Consider how relationships could be improved in each case.

Be prepared to feed back to the class.

Saying what you mean and meaning what you say!

Activity 3

Think of as many different ways as you can to say the word 'yes', so that each time it has a different meaning. Try saying it to yourself in your head as if you:

- really, really mean it
- are not sure if you mean it
- don't mean it at all.

Try out these different ways of saying 'yes' with a partner, but don't reveal which is which. Could they guess the different feelings or thoughts you were having as you said each one? How could they tell?

Our tone of voice, the expressions we use, the speed at which we speak – all of these affect how our words are heard. The way we say words can reveal different feelings or thoughts.

As with 'yes', the way we say 'no' to something can reveal our true feelings. Both what is said and how are important, for example, looking away, body freezing and shrugging might be ways that someone says 'no' to something. Source 2 shows some words that describe different ways of saying 'no'.

Source 2 Different ways to say 'no'

Let's take two of these words that people sometimes mistake for each other: 'aggressively' and 'assertively'. Here are some definitions to explain the difference:

Speaking aggressively:	**attacking**
	being hostile
	being offensive
Speaking assertively:	**declaring**
	being confident
	being sure

As you can see, speaking aggressively can make the person you are communicating with feel negative, and may not help you get your point across. On the other hand, speaking assertively helps to clearly communicate something, and can be very effective.

Is it easy to say 'no'?
- Does it depend on the person asking the question?
- What if you're trying to make someone else happy?
- What if there will be implications if you say no?
- What if there are implications if you say yes?
- Does saying no mean you're being rude?

Activity 4

Read the speech bubbles in Source 3. Which of these are examples of aggressive or assertive behaviour? Which of these might be 'passive'? What do you think 'passive' means?

Activity 5

Saying 'no' is not just verbal. We can use our facial expressions and body language. Prepare a five-second one-person role play where you say no: using your voice, your facial expressions and your body language.

Find a partner. Decide who is A and who is B. A performs their role play first. Your teacher will tell you when to start and stop. B watches A's performance and makes a note of the signals that they are getting from A. Then swap.

Be prepared to feed back to the class.

Activity 6

Reflect upon what you have learned today. Can you think of a time when you have had to be assertive? Maybe you had to tell a friend they were interrupting your learning and you would like to sit somewhere else in class? Maybe you had to tell an adult that you were worried about a young person's behaviour? Maybe you had to end a close relationship?

> Come on, let's skip class!

> Oh, alright then, if you think it will be OK?

> No! You are always doing the wrong thing! I don't want to be your friend anymore!

> No, I am going to class. I know that is what we should do.

Source 3 Aggressive or assertive?

By the end of 3.4 you will:

- know what happens in marriage and other partnership ceremonies, and be able to discuss the significance of commitment vows
- be able to explain the legal status of marriage, civil partnerships and other types of long-term relationships
- be able to give some reasons why stable relationships may support the bringing up of children.

Starter

The Scottish Government says it is important for people your age to learn about marriage and other types of stable relationships. Why do you think this was included in a list of topics that schools should cover?

People may feel they are happiest when their lives are stable, when they know they can depend and rely on the people around them. Many people choose to live their lives as part of a couple.

How important is a stable relationship in bringing up children? What are the roles and responsibilities of parents or carers in raising children?

Activity 1

Think about people you see on television or have read about online or in books who live together in couples. Give some examples. For each example, answer the following questions:
1 Why do you think they have chosen to be together?
2 What do you think makes them happier being together than being alone?

When two people live together as discussed in Activity 1, we talk about them having made a 'commitment' to each other. Some people choose to show their commitment to and love for another person by taking part in a ceremony. Marriage and civil partnership ceremonies are two examples of these as shown in the photos below.

Source 1 People celebrate their marriages or civil partnerships by making an act of commitment to each other.

How does the legal status of marriage, civil partnerships and other types of long-term relationships differ?

A civil partnership is a legally recognised relationship between two people and offers many of the same benefits as a conventional marriage. Those in a civil partnership benefit from the same rights as married couples in terms of tax benefits, pensions and inheritance.

Marriage and civil partnerships are legally binding and can only be ended if one partner dies, or by applying to court to bring the partnership or marriage legally to an end. In the case of marriage, this is called divorce.

Vows are special promises that people make at important times in their lives. At a marriage or civil partnership ceremony, the two people repeat vows to each other.

Activity 2

Source 3 shows modern vows people may use in a Christian marriage ceremony. People often write their own vows. Write your own version of a set of marriage or civil partnership vows. Decide what you think is important for two people to promise to each other. Think about what is needed to keep a relationship healthy. Consider the importance of commitment and stability in raising any children.

Seven vows in a Hindu wedding

1 The first vow says: the bride and the groom will provide prosperity as a household to the family and will stand against those who try to get in the way.

2 The second vow says: the bride and the groom will lead a healthy life by developing their physical, mental and spiritual wellbeing.

3 The third vow says: the couple will earn a living by proper means, so that their materialistic wealth increases well.

4 The fourth vow says: the married couple will respect, love and understand each other and will acquire knowledge, happiness and harmony.

5 The fifth vow says: the couple will expand their family by having healthy, brave and honest children, for whom they will be responsible.

6 The sixth vow says: the bride and the groom will have self-control of the mind, body and soul, and will have a long marital relationship.

7 The seventh and the last vow says: they promise that they will be true and loyal to each other and will remain companions, and will be the best of friends for their lifetime.

Source 2

In a Scottish, Christian religious ceremony, the details of vows are often created by the couple being married after discussion by the minister/celebrant taking the ceremony. These vows must include a declaration by both bride and groom that they accept each other as husband and wife (or accept each other in marriage). Below is an example of modern vows. The bride and groom face each other, take each other's hands and, one at a time, say:

I, ... now take you, ...

to be my wife/husband.

In the presence of God

and before these witnesses

I promise to be

a loving

faithful

and loyal husband/wife to you

as long as we both shall live.

Source 3

How do people show love and commitment?

Activity 3

Look at the photos in Source 1 on page 26 and Source 4 below and the different vows in Sources 2 and 3. List the things that people do in marriage and civil partnership ceremonies to demonstrate their love and commitment to each other.

Signing the register makes the marriage/partnership legal.

Kissing at the wedding ceremony celebrates the couple's happiness.

Many people celebrate their weddings as part of a religious ceremony. This is from a Hindu wedding.

Source 4

Exchanging rings and making promises to each other form part of most weddings. This is a Jewish 'ketubah' – a marriage contract.

Activity 4

Just because two people are in a committed relationship doesn't stop things going wrong. Look again at these words:

for better, for worse,

for richer, for poorer,

in sickness and in health

Why should couples think about the ups and downs of being in a relationship before they have their ceremony?

What is the legal age for getting married?

In Scotland, you can get married from the age of 16, with or without parental consent. In England, Wales and Northern Ireland, you can get married from the age of 16, if you have parental consent. If you don't have parental consent, you cannot get married until 18.

Forced marriages

A forced marriage is where a person is put under emotional pressure, or exposed to violence or sexual abuse to accept a marriage proposal. In 2006, the Home Office Minister Baroness Scotland stated that 'forced marriage is an abuse of human rights and a form of domestic violence which cannot be justified on religious or cultural grounds.'

A forced marriage is different to an arranged marriage because, in an arranged marriage, there is a choice and consent from both people. If anyone is found guilty of forcing someone into marriage they can be prosecuted for kidnap, false imprisonment or rape. People who are forced into marriage can feel very lonely and believe that there is no escape from their situation. However, help, advice, information and support are available so they need to try to speak out and not put up with something which clearly goes against their human rights. A person has a right to choose who they wish to marry and has a right not to be forced into something they do not want to do.

Remember: a forced marriage can include a wide range of pressures applied to an individual. They might be physical, psychological, sexual, financial or emotional pressures, or involve abuse (both emotional and physical), or harassment. If an individual felt that they didn't have a choice in saying 'no', or that they would not have consented if pressure wasn't placed on them, then this is deemed as 'forced'.

The Forced Marriage Unit

The Foreign and Commonwealth Office has set up a unit called 'The Forced Marriage Unit', which has a helpline staffed by trained professionals who can give advice and help to anyone who has been forced into marriage overseas, or who is at risk of being forced into marriage. They can also provide advice and support for people who may be worried about relatives and friends who are victims of forced marriages.

Activity 5

Go back to one of the couples you thought about in Activity 1. If you could give them one piece of good advice about marriage or civil partnership, what would it be?

By the end of 3.5 you will:
- be able to say what 'abuse' is
- be able to identify strategies for dealing with potentially dangerous situations.

Starter

'A problem shared is a problem halved.'

There are times when you need to talk to someone. This may not be easy as the subject might be sensitive or you could feel that you are telling on someone. A friend may have told you something and you feel you should report it. You are not gossiping – there is a risk that your friend is in a potentially dangerous situation.

With a partner, discuss who you could talk to. Who could offer support and advice? Be prepared to feed back to the class.

What is abuse?

Sometimes people might try to force you to do things you don't want to do. Or they might lead you towards situations in which you want to please someone but end up doing something you don't want to do. We call what this other person is doing to you 'abuse'.

No one has the right to hurt you or make you do anything that feels wrong, but it's not always easy to know if you, or someone you know, is being abused.

Abuse can be many different things: verbal, emotional, physical or sexual. The most important thing to know is that abuse of any kind in any relationship is never the fault of the person who is being abused. There are four main kinds of abuse:

Verbal abuse

Someone threatening you or calling you nasty names. For example, someone who shouts at you all the time to make you feel bad.

Emotional abuse (coercive control)

Someone using their power to manipulate and control you. You might feel scared to do something in case it upsets them, or they might constantly check up on you or demand to know where you are all the time.

Physical abuse

Someone physically hurting you in any way (by hitting or slapping you, for example).

Sexual abuse

Someone forcing you into sexual activity you don't want or threatening you if you do not have sexual contact with them (this includes kissing and touching, not just intercourse).

Remember what makes a healthy relationship: fairness/equality (give-and-take); trust; honesty; respect; communication. In a good relationship, both people want what's best for each other.

Unfortunately, not all relationships are healthy.
- Some people make you think they are your friend, boyfriend or girlfriend, but really they might be just using you.
- Some people make young people feel special (for example, giving them gifts or paying them compliments) in order to gain control over them.
- Some people use pressure and threats to try to gain control over others.

Some types of behaviour within relationships are criminal, including violent behaviour, abuse, sexual exploitation and grooming, and coercive control. (Coercive control means when someone uses threats, violence and other abuse in order to control another person.) Victims of these types of behaviour in relationships should be supported to report it to the police. The behaviour will have a negative effect on the victim's mental health and their ability to go about their day-to-day tasks: which might include school or work. It will also affect the relationships that the victim has with other people now, and in the future.

Stranger = danger. Does it?

Many young people have been made aware of the possible danger of strangers. But we know from reports that most abuse is carried out by a family member, a friend or someone the family trusts. If the abuser is not a stranger it may feel even more scary to speak out and say something.

Source 1 What is 'abuse'?

Activity 1

Imagine this situation: You are fairly sure, from things they have said and the way they are behaving, that one of your friends is being abused in some way.
- How could you support them in getting the right help?
- What if your friend tells you something bad is happening to them but they think it's their own fault, so they are worried about getting help. What would you say to them?
- They are afraid to even talk much about it because they are afraid of what will happen. Who can you encourage them to talk to without fear or worry?
- Should the police ever be involved?

Use Source 2 to help you support your friend.

You need to be able to recognise when a relationship is unhealthy and have the courage to talk to someone if you are worried. Healthy relationships enrich our lives and make us feel good.

Child sexual exploitation

'Child sexual exploitation (CSE) is a type of sexual abuse. Children in exploitative situations and relationships receive something such as gifts, money or affection as a result of performing sexual activities or others performing sexual activities on them.

Children or young people may be tricked into believing they're in a loving, consensual relationship. They might be invited to parties and given drugs and alcohol. They may also be 'groomed' and exploited online.

Some children and young people are trafficked into or within the UK for the purpose of sexual exploitation. Sexual exploitation can also happen to young people in gangs.'

NSPCC

Source 3 Child sexual exploitation

It is important to remember that abuse of any kind is unacceptable. If you feel you have experienced any form of abuse then you need to talk to someone. Think back to the starter activity. Who could you talk to?

For advice online, visit: www.brook.org.uk/topics/abuse-and-violence.

Activity 2

A friend asks you to cover for them. They met someone online who they are going to meet face-to-face for the first time. They don't want anyone to know. What's your response?

✓ You have the right to be safe. You will not be punished if you tell someone you feel unsafe or threatened in any way by anyone.

✓ You should always seek help if you feel uncomfortable, confused or scared. You will never be blamed for telling the truth.

✓ Your body is your own. Don't let anyone touch you where you don't want to be touched.

✓ Say 'no': you don't have to hug or kiss anyone if you don't want to.

✓ Abusers and bullies often say 'it's our secret'. This isn't the truth.

✓ No harm will come to you or your loved ones if you tell the truth about abuse.

Source 2 Personal safety: your rights. Adapted with permission from Brook

Activity 3

How can you tell when a situation is unsafe, and set boundaries about what you want to do and don't want to do? How can you tell if someone wants a relationship with you for the right or wrong reasons?

Activity 4

Think of one person who you like to spend time with. Why is this person special to you? Do they make you laugh? Do you share the same interests? Do they listen to you? Do they support you when you need help?

By the end of 4.1 you will:

- be able to give reasons why people have sex
- understand your choices around sex
- be able to explain some of the issues surrounding 'early sex'.

Starter

In pairs, consider what sex is and why people have it. Look at Source 1. These are possible reasons why people have sex. Do you agree with any of these? Do you disagree with any? Are there any other reasons?

Be prepared to feed back to the class.

Activity 1

In pairs, discuss the signs or situations, thoughts or feelings that may mean a couple are ready to have sex.

Be prepared to feed your thoughts back to the class. As a class, define some boundaries. For example, there must be mutual respect, open communication, awareness of choice.

Activity 2

Look at the phrases in Source 2. What do you think the people saying these things are trying to achieve? Think of some possible responses to the statements.

Look at Source 3. Sometimes young people might want others to think that they are more sexually experienced than they are. Why is this?

People have sex because:

- They want to have a baby.
- They love each other.
- It gives them pleasure.
- They want to show each other how much they love each other.
- It reinforces love in a marriage.
- Having sex is always part of being in a relationship.
- They 'fancy' each other.

Source 1 Why do people have sex?

You would if you loved me!

But it's the natural thing to do!

Everyone is doing it!

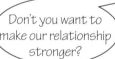
Don't you want to make our relationship stronger?

You'll have to do it sometime – why not now, with me?

Do you want to be a virgin all your life?

But Maya said you would be up for it!

I'll only put it in for a second ...

Source 2 Please?!

Yeah, I've had sex lots of times ...

I lost it when I was thirteen ...

It's amazing – you don't know what you're missing!

You're a virgin, you wouldn't understand ...

You mean you've *never* done it?!?

Nobody will be interested in you if they hear you're frigid.

Source 3 Good reasons?

Activity 3

Read Source 4. What advice would you give Kojo, Rach, Bailey and Sam?

1 Kojo

Kojo met Sandi at the club. They've been together for over a month. The two of them get on really well and Kojo's mates have accepted Sandi as a good friend too. When they've spent time alone there's been a lot of kissing but that's as far as things have gone. Recently Sandi has been suggesting they take things further – but Kojo doesn't feel ready to do this ...

2 Rach

Rach is 13 and her parents are letting her have her fourteenth birthday party at home. They are going out for the evening and leaving Rach's older brothers, Nick and Dan, in charge. During the party, Nick and Dan are upstairs watching a DVD. Downstairs, Michael, who really fancies Rach, suggests they go up to her room – no one will notice. Rach fancies him too but this isn't what she wants.

3 Bailey

Bailey and Gabe have been going out for six months now, since the start of Third year (S3). Bailey really likes Gabe and enjoys every minute that they are together. They share many of the same interests and kiss and cuddle when they are alone together. Gabe isn't pushy but Bailey feels that Gabe would like to take things further. However, Bailey is worried about not having any sexual feelings for Gabe. Bailey is concerned that this is not normal.

4 Sam

Sam is in the same English class as Reese. Reese is very good looking and is a popular member of the class. Sam has had a crush on Reese since they found themselves sitting next to each other: the teacher had a seating plan! However, Sam knows that Reese has had a few partners in the past and is worried that there might be an expectation to have sex if they get together.

Source 4 Choices

The law states people need to be 16 years old before they can choose to have a sexual relationship – not that this means you *have* to have sex when you're 16. Despite all the gossip we might hear and what we read on the internet, the majority of young people in this country do wait until they are 16 or older to have sex.

'Early sex' can be defined as having sex before the age of 16.

The law is the same for those in same sex relationships.

Activity 4

Imagine two young people like those in Source 5 are trying to decide whether to have or to delay having early sex. What reasons might they come up with in each case? What would they need to consider? Do this activity on your own.

Source 5 A couple in love

By the end of 4.2 you will:

- be able to explain how pornography affects lives
- be able to identify the risks and implications of sexting.

Starter

In pairs, you have one minute to brainstorm: what do you know or have you heard about 'pornography'?

Be prepared to share your thoughts with the class.

Pornography: a definition

'Pornography' is defined as: printed or visual material containing the explicit description or display of sexual organs or activity, intended to stimulate sexual excitement.

The word 'pornography' is often shortened to 'porn'.

Porn is any material (words, sounds, pictures) designed to be sexually arousing. Anatomical pictures (the kind you might find in medical information) may be sexually explicit, but are not intended to be arousing. That's the difference. Pornography has been around for a long time, but what has changed is how accessible it is, and its content. Your grandparents probably thought of it as top-shelf magazines or under-the-counter videos. In the past, people could see explicit images easily – but still not as immediately as at the click of a mouse.

There is now a huge volume of pornography at the click of a button, which although not intended for those under the age of 18, might be accessed by some young people. In fact, the age at which some young people first look at porn is getting lower.

Activity 1

Read Source 1. In pairs, discuss these concerns. Should we be concerned? Is there anything else that we should be concerned about?

Be prepared to feed back to the class.

We live in a society where so much is based around beautiful people in situations suggesting a connection with sex. More and more adverts tell you the perfume or deodorant you use, or the type of car

Porn changes how we feel about ourselves and about sex. It's easy to feel inadequate: some bodies are hairy and wobbly, not super tanned and perfectly toned …

If watching porn makes you feel weird inside, unhappy, confused or upset – then don't watch it.

People can become addicted to porn. They need to watch/read/see/listen to more and more to get pleasure from it. This eventually numbs the sense of pleasure and has a negative effect on mental wellbeing.

Porn is fantasy. We need to separate out truth (real people) from fantasy (actors).

Porn influences how we behave. Many images show girls being used just for the enjoyment of others. In reality no woman wants this to happen.

Young people consider porn as commonplace and so this can lead to risky sexual behaviour, both on and offline.

Source 1 Why should we be concerned?

you drive, will make other people fancy you. Look at music videos and the way people dress, gesture and dance, and the words they sing. They can often give the impression that the only thing young people are interested in is sex.

When sexual images are used in all sorts of media, it is not surprising that many people start to see such images as normal and ordinary. It's even been suggested that teenagers take this so much for granted that they don't think twice before putting revealing or risky photographs on their social networking pages. Some young people have sent nude or sexual photos to another person. This is called 'sexting'.

> Suzie and Rajiv started going out last year. They were crazy about each other and spent ages talking on the phone and texting. They'd take selfies blowing kisses to each other and text those too.
>
> A couple of months ago Rajiv suggested that they send each other special 'private' photos. Rajiv sent a topless one so Suzie copied him and sent one back.
>
> Two weeks ago, they split up. Yesterday Tom, Rajiv's best mate, stopped Suzie in the street, pointed to her breasts and said, 'Nice breasts, Suzie.'
>
> Suzie thought straight away that Tom must have seen the photo. She went straight round to Rajiv's and had a go at him about it. He admitted it but couldn't see why she was so upset. 'It was only a joke!' he said. 'Anyway, I put it online two days ago and you didn't say anything then.'

Source 3 Suzie's story

A few years ago, most people only took a camera to special occasions. Now most people carry cameras all the time – on mobile phones. They can take photos anywhere and share them in no time. Photos can be a great way to show your friends what you're up to.

But remember, it can be really hard, sometimes impossible, to delete photos from other people's mobiles. Once you've shared something on your mobile you've lost control of it – it can be copied, shared and even edited! If you send an embarrassing photo to a friend, it could end up anywhere! Would you want your mum, gran, teacher or future employer to see it? If the answer is 'no', then don't send it.

Creating or sharing naked or 'sexy' photos of anyone under 18 is illegal, even if the person doing so is also under 18.

Activity 4

Remember – it's never too late to get help if you've shared something you regret. Seek help from an adult you trust. Can you think of anyone else who could help? Think of a slogan that will remind young people of the implications of 'sexting'.

A recent NSPCC survey (www.childrenscommissioner. gov.uk/wp-content/ uploads/2017/06/MDX-NSPCC-OCC-Online-Pornography-Report.pdf) into the impact of online pornography on the values, attitudes, beliefs and behaviours of children showed that 53 per cent of boys and 39 per cent of girls saw it as a realistic depiction of sex.

Source 2 Reality vs fantasy

Activity 2

Online pornography can affect:
- how people view themselves
- how people view relationships.

How does the reality differ from the fantasy? What makes a healthy relationship?

Discuss in pairs. Be prepared to feed back to the class.

Activity 3

Read Source 3 and discuss the following questions:
1. Did Rajiv break any law:
   a when he sent the photo on to Tom?
   b when he posted it online?
2. Who does sending these 'private' types of photos affect?
3. What can Suzie do?
4. What are the other risks if someone takes nude or sexual photos and texts them or posts them online?

By the end of 4.3 you will:
- be able to explain 'consent' and why it is so important
- be able to state some laws around sex.

Starter

Ash and Nick meet at the skateboard park. They get along really well from the start as they have so much in common. They catch up every time they go to the park but then start to meet more often: Ash meets Nick from school some days; they call each other; and they text each other constantly. They enjoy being together. They like to chat, hold hands and kiss. Ash starts buying Nick presents. At first, just treats like chocolates but then the presents become more expensive. After a couple of weeks, Ash asks Nick for sex.

Come up with three questions that you want to ask about the situation. Write them clearly on a piece of paper and pass them to your teacher. Do not put your name on the piece of paper.

Activity 1

Read Source 1. What are the key messages here? Be prepared to feed back to the class.

The definition of consent is 'an agreement which is given willingly and freely without exploitation, threat or fear, and by a person who has the capacity to give their agreement.'

Exactly. The person giving consent shouldn't be scared or threatened, or feel manipulated or exploited. And the word 'capacity' is important too – for example, you can't say yes to something if you're unconscious …

So it's not just about saying 'yes', or 'no' then – the words 'willingly and freely' show that the person giving consent should be enthusiastic, and know what they're saying yes to – it's more about informed consent …

Of course! It sounds like both people need to be agreed on what they're doing – they shouldn't be confused, they both need to be on the same page, but I think it's important too to keep checking.

Yeah – the person asking for consent is really responsible for checking this, and for not putting the other person under pressure.

True – because people can change their minds – you can say yes to something when it's started, but during it you might want to stop, and that's ok. I think that's true whatever you're doing, whether in real life or online too.

Source 1 What is consent?

Think back to the starter activity. How easy is it for Nick to say no? Remember: key concepts in a 'healthy relationship' are mutual respect and trust. A healthy relationship can be contrasted with an unhealthy relationship – an unequal relationship without mutual respect and sharing, where one person has more power or control and manipulates or takes advantage of the other.

There are laws against coercion and grooming. If someone repeatedly asks for consent and it is refused, that can count as sexual harassment. Remember that you never have to do something that you feel is unsafe and you should never be put under any pressure to have sex.

If someone forces someone to have sex, that is rape, even if the young people are of similar age. A court may choose to give a life sentence when someone is convicted of rape.

Under 16s' access to sexual health services

Under 16s can get access to contraception and sexual and reproductive health services. Consent from parents or carers is not legally necessary and your parent/carer will not be contacted, unless there is a risk of harm to yourself, or others, which will be discussed with you first.

Young people have the right to the same duties of care and confidentiality as adults. Confidentiality can only be broken if the health, safety or welfare of the young person, or others, is in any way at risk.

However, if the young person is under 13, nurses and health workers may feel it is in their best interest to involve other people, such as a parent, carer or social worker, as under 13s cannot legally consent to any sexual activity.

Sexual images, age and the law

It is illegal to create or share sexual imagery of anyone under the age of 18, even if you are the person in the picture.

You must remember that though the age of sexual consent is 16, sending sexual imagery of anyone under 18 is illegal. The law that makes it illegal to take or share indecent images of children was created to protect young people from sexual abuse. It was not intended to make children into criminals. Nonetheless, where police have been notified, the incident will be listed as a 'crime' and the young person involved will be a 'suspect'.

Sexual consent, age and the law

The law states:

- The legal age of consent to sexual activity is 16. Consent is defined in law as agreement by choice made by someone with the freedom and capacity to consent.
- Under the law, it is the person seeking consent who is responsible for ensuring that these conditions are met.

The law is there to protect children from abuse or exploitation, rather than to prosecute under-16s who consent to have sex with each other. The legal age of consent is 16 but not all young people are ready to have sex at 16 and many will choose to wait for the right time.

The law says anyone under the age of 13 can never legally give consent.

Activity 2

Write down in your own words what is meant by 'consent'. Why is knowing what is meant by 'consent' so important, and how can you be sure that consent has been given?

By the end of 4.4 you will:
- be able to explain the link between lifestyle and fertility
- understand how fertilisation leads to pregnancy and birth
- be able to identify choices around pregnancy.

Starter

Work in pairs. Write the three headings: Conception; Pregnancy; Birth. Brainstorm as much as you can under each heading. Be prepared to feed back to the class.

During puberty, our bodies start to produce hormones that make us feel different from before. These hormones might lead to sexual feelings. Also, our bodies change physically so that when we are aged 16 or over, we can have sexual intercourse if we want to. Sexual intercourse can lead to conception, pregnancy and birth. This is called 'human reproduction'.

Activity 1

Human reproduction usually follows the same pattern. Look at Source 1. Describe the sequence that leads up to, and includes, the birth of a baby.

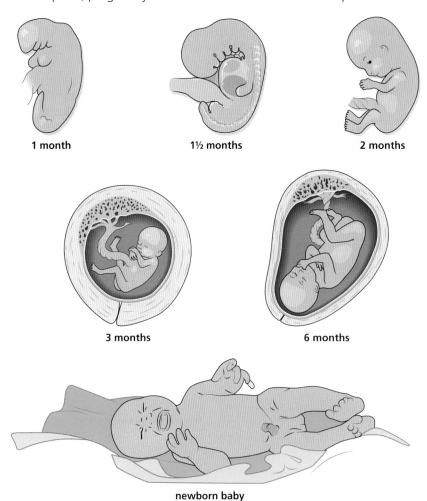

1 month   1½ months   2 months

3 months   6 months

newborn baby

Source 1 A baby develops: first, the foetus attaches itself to the wall of the uterus. Over the next nine months it grows and develops into a baby. The baby is born.

Ectopic pregnancy, molar pregnancy and miscarriage

Unfortunately, some pregnancies do not go as planned. Sometimes an ectopic or molar pregnancy can happen (see Source 2). Miscarriages are also fairly common. This is when the embryo or foetus dies a natural death during pregnancy. Many miscarriages don't have a known cause, but reasons include:

- the foetus doesn't develop normally and can't survive
- the placenta isn't supplied with enough blood
- developing a high fever or particular illness
- an irregular shaped uterus (womb), or growths in the uterus which don't leave enough room for the baby to grow.

Fertility and lifestyle

Humans are closely tuned into their surroundings – especially when it comes to making babies. Just as with other animals, our bodies only reach the peak of fertility when conditions seem right for raising babies. If there's any sign of illness, malnourishment or an unhealthy environment, our bodies may decide to put parenthood on hold. Adults wanting to start a family are usually given this advice:

- maintain a healthy weight (that is neither overweight or underweight)
- exercise regularly
- eat a healthy diet (a lack of nutrients such as Vitamin C, zinc and folic acid can slow sperm production in men)
- don't smoke and limit the amount of alcohol you drink
- stay clear of recreational drugs and check your prescribed drugs.

On the whole, the best plan for protecting fertility looks very like the basic strategy for good health: watch your weight, exercise, eat well, and avoid smoking and heavy drinking. These habits are good for anyone, whether planning a family now or in the future!

Some sexually transmitted infections also affect fertility. However, there are many causes of infertility, and fertility problems, where it is impossible to identify the cause.

Common causes of infertility include:

- lack of regular ovulation (the monthly release of an egg)
- blocked or damaged fallopian tubes (can be caused by a past infection)
- endometriosis (where tissue that behaves like the lining of the womb is found outside the womb)
- poor-quality sperm.

The fertilised egg develops in the fallopian tube. There is no room for the foetus to grow and surgery is needed to remove it.

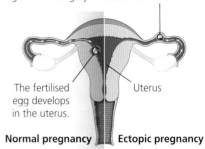

The fertilised egg develops in the uterus.

Uterus

Normal pregnancy | **Ectopic pregnancy**

Ectopic pregnancy

An abnormal fertilised egg develops in the uterus and the placenta cells grow too quickly and leave no room for the foetus to grow.

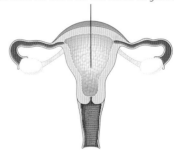

Molar pregnancy

Molar pregnancy

Source 2 Ectopic and molar pregnancies

Activity 2

What makes a healthy lifestyle? Work in pairs and then feed back to the class.

Choices around pregnancy

There are generally three choices for someone who is pregnant:

1 give birth to the baby and raise the baby

2 give birth to the baby and place the baby up for adoption

3 end the pregnancy by having an abortion.

Age, values, beliefs, health, current situation and future goals all play a role in the decision. The decision might also be limited by how advanced the pregnancy is.

Generally, adoption happens shortly after a baby is born. The person who has given birth to the baby signs legally binding documents which mean they have no further rights to the child. The other parent, if known, also signs the consent forms.

The most common type of surgical abortion is called 'vacuum aspiration'. This can take place up to the fourteenth week of pregnancy, and will happen in a health care provider's office or clinic. After the fourteenth week of pregnancy, the abortion procedure is called a 'dilation and evacuation' (D&E). A D&E procedure can be done in a health care provider's office, clinic or hospital. It takes longer than a vacuum aspiration and it might mean the woman has to visit the clinic more than once. Abortion can also be caused by taking certain prescribed drugs – this is called a 'medical abortion' – and cannot take place after nine weeks of pregnancy.

There is a wide range of free and confidential sexual health advice and services for young people. They may be listed as sexual health clinics or family planning clinics. Brook is a provider which offers free and confidential sexual health advice and services specifically for young people under 25. (**www.brook.org.uk/our-work/education-on-pregnancy-choices-and-abortion**)

Fertility treatment

Fertility treatment is used for those couples or individuals who cannot conceive a child naturally. There are many reasons why a person may struggle to have children, for example: they have problems with their reproductive organs; they may be in a same sex relationship; or they have passed their 'child-bearing' age. Nowadays, pregnancy can also happen through 'assisted conception', sometimes called 'in vitro' fertilisation.

IVF – in vitro fertilisation: *In vitro* is Latin and means 'in glass'. This is when an egg is fertilised by a sperm outside the human body. This is done with the help of medical experts. The egg and sperm are put together in a test tube with the hope that a sperm will fertilise the egg. If and when an embryo forms, it is then carefully placed back into the uterus to grow naturally.

Activity 3

In pairs, discuss the three choices available:
- giving birth to the baby and raising it
- giving birth to the baby and placing it for adoption
- ending the pregnancy by having an abortion.

Discuss how age, values, beliefs, health, current situation, and future goals play a role in making the decision. Be prepared to feed back to the class.

Artificial insemination: This is when sperm is collected and placed into the uterus using artificial methods. This is to increase the chance of the egg being fertilised by the sperm and therefore a baby being created.

Artificial insemination takes place in two ways:

1 The sperm will come from the person's partner.

2 If the partner has unhealthy sperm or the person doesn't have a partner then the sperm will come from a donor who is anonymous (the identity of the donor is not revealed to the parent but can be accessed by any children that are conceived when they are 18).

Carol and David

Carol and David have been together a long time. They have both had very busy lives and so it wasn't until Carol was 40 that they even thought about starting a family. However, after a couple of years of trying, they have had no luck.

Hannah

Hannah has had several miscarriages. She and her husband, Levi, have been for fertility tests and have been told that they both have lower than average fertility. They are desperate for a baby.

Mark and Ben

Mark and Ben got married a few years ago. They feel that their 'family' is not yet complete.

Esther

Esther wants a baby. She has no partner and has no intention of having a partner. She has always been very independent and knows that she can raise a child on her own.

Activity 4

Read the stories opposite. What advice would you give?

Activity 5

Some people choose to start a family by adopting a baby or child. The new adoptive parent(s) agree to raise the child as their own. They sign a legal adoption document, following a lengthy adoption process.
- With your partner you have ten minutes to write a list of all the checks and information you think are involved in the lengthy process of adoption.
- What would adoption agencies want to know?

This activity will help you consider what you think should happen before making the decision to start a family. How important is it that children are raised in a stable environment?

Activity 6

You have received a lot of information about conception, pregnancy and birth. Think of one piece of key advice that you would give to a young couple who are considering starting a family.

By the end of 4.5 you will:
- be able to identify some facts and myths about contraception
- be able to name a variety of types of contraception
- be able to give advice to young people wanting to learn about contraception.

Starter

You already know that 'conception' is the joining together of an egg cell and sperm cell at fertilisation, and the implanting of these cells in the uterus to start a pregnancy. So, what do you think 'contraception' means?

Work in pairs and agree upon a definition for the word 'contraception'.

1 The 'pill'	2 'If we do it standing up it'll be fine.'	3 IUS/IUD
4 'It'll never happen to me.'	5 Emergency contraceptive pills	6 'It'll be OK the first time.'
7 Contraceptive injection	8 Using clingfilm	9 Pulling out before coming/ ejaculating
10 Having sex during a period	11 No sexual touching	12 Implant

Source 1 Which of these methods protect against pregnancy?

Condoms (picture F in Source 2) work as a simple and effective contraceptive to protect against pregnancy and STIs. However, condoms are only really effective if they are used properly. A condom is made of very thin latex (rubber) or polyurethane and fits over the erect penis. It acts as a barrier as it covers the whole of the penis and stops sexual fluids being exchanged. A new condom should be used each time a person has sexual contact.

Before using condoms, it's important to check:
- that the packet has a BSI or CE Kite mark, which shows it's been safety tested
- the instructions in the packet, which have diagrams showing how to use the condoms properly
- that the condom is in date, they have expiry dates printed on the packet, and the packet is not damaged.

Activity 1

1. Working with a partner, look at Source 1 to the left and decide which of these methods protect against pregnancy.
2. Now see if you can match a picture from Source 2 opposite to any of the genuine methods of contraception in Source 1.
3. Do any of these methods of contraception also protect against sexually transmitted infections (STIs)?

Activity 2

Condoms are 98 per cent effective when they are used correctly. They can protect against pregnancy and sexually transmitted infections (STIs). What are the correct facts about how to use a condom?

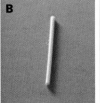

Source 2 Contraceptives

Activity 3

Roz and Ike are both sixteen. They've been going out for just about a year. They haven't had sex yet – they are thinking about it but have some questions they want answered first. They are planning to go to their local sexual health clinic. Can you help answer their questions?

If we go to the clinic for advice before having sex won't they think we're wasting their time?

We've heard that clinics keep things confidential. Is it true that they won't tell anybody else?

The clinic is a long way from where we live. Can we go to see the doctor instead?

Will either of us have to have a physical examination before getting contraception?

Do we have to pay for the advice and the contraceptives?

Are free contraceptives as reliable as the ones you can buy?

Which contraceptives also help prevent sexually transmitted infections (STIs)?

Source 3 Roz and Ike

You can check your advice to Roz and Ike against the information online.

Visit: **www.brook.org.uk/your-life/category/contraception**.

Or pick up leaflets about local health services: these can usually be found in your local library, GP practices, clinics, hospitals and at young people's services.

Activity 4

Roz and Ike still have quite a lot to learn and there are so many things they are worried about. Would it be better for them to wait before having sex? Reflect upon this question.

By the end of 4.6 you will:
- be able to explain facts about key sexually transmitted infections (STIs).

Starter

How do you think a person could tell whether or not they had a sexually transmitted infection (STI)?

STIs are mainly transmitted (passed from one person to another) during sex. There are at least 25 types of STI with a range of different symptoms.

Activity 1

In pairs, decide whether you agree with, disagree with or are not sure about the statements in the STI quiz in Source 1.

1 Among teenagers in the UK, chlamydia is the most common STI.
2 If you use a condom you are protected against STIs.
3 You can get an STI from a toilet seat.
4 There is a cure for every STI.
5 If it hurts when you pee, you have definitely got an STI.
6 STIs can make you infertile.
7 If you sleep around a lot you will get an STI.
8 You can't have more than one STI at a time.
9 If someone has an STI they are only infectious when they have symptoms.
10 The only way to find out if you have an STI is to get tested.

Source 1 STI quiz – agree or disagree?

Source 2 gives you some information about the six most important STIs to be aware of. These are the ones most likely to be transmitted among young people – and some have serious consequences.

Chlamydia
Symptoms: Most people don't have any symptoms for a long time
Effects: Left untreated can cause infertility
Treatment: Antibiotic

Genital warts
Symptoms: Growths or warts in the genital area; they can take a year to appear after infection
Effects: Can be uncomfortable
Treatment: Ointments or freezing (done by medical professionals)

Herpes
Symptoms: Small painful blisters or sores which heal in a week or two
Effects: Painful when outbreaks of sores occur
Treatment: No cure but tablets and cream can reduce the severity

Pubic lice (or crabs)
Symptoms: Pubic lice are not necessarily sexually transmitted but are usually passed on through close body contact; they can cause severe itching
Effects: No long-term health problems – but will disappear only if treated
Treatment: Special lotions which can be bought in pharmacies

Gonorrhoea
Symptoms: Most women and some men don't have any symptoms
Effects: Left untreated can cause problems including infertility
Treatment: Antibiotics

Syphilis
Symptoms: Sometimes none, sometimes a painless sore may appear within nine to ninety days, followed later by a rash and flu-like symptoms
Effects: If untreated may cause serious permanent health problems such as damage to the nervous system/dementia
Treatment: Antibiotics

Source 2 STI information

Chlamydia

Chlamydia is the most common sexually transmitted infection (STI) in the UK and is most common in under 25s. Here are some key facts:

- There are often no signs or symptoms.
- It can affect anyone who has ever had unprotected sex.
- 1 in 10 young people who are sexually active are thought to have chlamydia.
- It is a bacterial infection.
- Tests usually involve giving a urine sample or taking a swab, both of which are very easy.
- If left untreated it can affect fertility.
- It is passed on through unprotected vaginal, anal or oral sex, sharing sex toys or genital-to-genital contact.
- The only way to protect yourself is to use condoms every time you have sex.
- It is treated with antibiotics.

Chlamydia is sometimes described as a 'silent' infection due to the fact about 50 per cent of people with the infection don't have any obvious signs or symptoms. So even if you don't have any symptoms, it's really important you go to be tested for STIs if you've had unprotected sex. Unprotected sex means you haven't used a barrier method of contraception, for example, a condom or dental dam (a latex sheet that can be used between the mouth and the other person's genitals during oral sex).

If you leave chlamydia untreated it can spread to other parts of the body, causing pain and inflammation. There are risks of developing pelvic inflammatory disease (PID) and suffering damage to the fallopian tubes for those with female bodies, and an infection in the testicles for those with male bodies.

If you do have symptoms, they can often take a few weeks to appear and you might notice:

- unusual discharge from the vagina, penis or rectum
- burning and itching in the genital area (men)
- pain when peeing
- heavy periods or bleeding between periods
- pelvic and lower abdominal pain
- abdominal pain in women during vaginal sex
- bleeding during or after sex
- painful swelling of testicles.

Source 3 1 in 10 young people who are sexually active are thought to have chlamydia

HIV and AIDs

Human	Only affects people
Immunodeficiency	Stops the immune system working properly
Virus	A living cell that can transmit infections
Acquired	Does not occur naturally – you get it from someone or somewhere else
Immune	The body system that fights illness and infections
Deficiency	Not fully functioning or working
Syndrome	A collection of illnesses or conditions

Source 4 HIV and AIDS

The red ribbon has been an international symbol of HIV for over twenty years. World AIDS Day, December each year, is a chance to show support for the 40 million people living with HIV worldwide.

Many famous people, such as Sir Elton John, work hard to promote HIV and AIDS awareness.

Activity 2

1 Read Source 4 about HIV and AIDS.
2 Look at statements a–j below and sort them into three groups:
   ✓ True
   ✗ Untrue
   ? Uncertain
   a HIV only affects gay men and people who inject illegal drugs.
   b More than 100 000 people in the UK (nearly 6000 in Scotland) are living with HIV.
   c You can become infected with HIV if you share food and cutlery with someone who has the virus.
   d The red ribbon is an international symbol of support for people living with HIV and AIDS.
   e HIV is increasing in every region of the world.
   f You cannot get HIV from swimming pools.
   g HIV and AIDS cannot be cured.
   h People living with HIV can expect a near normal life span if they are diagnosed promptly.
   i Someone with HIV who is pregnant will always pass HIV to the baby in the womb, on delivery or while breastfeeding.
   j If you have unprotected sex with someone who has HIV, you will definitely get infected.

HIV and AIDS affect people across the world.

Source 5 World AIDS Day

Activity 3

Read Source 6 where you will learn that Lily has been diagnosed with HIV. However, she is dealing with her diagnosis in a positive way.

How has Lily been able to remain so positive? What does she mean by 'knowledge is power'? What does the future look like for Lily?

"MY BOYFRIEND OF THREE YEARS AND I PLAN TO REMAIN TOGETHER AND HAVE CHILDREN ONCE I HAVE FINISHED UNIVERSITY"

I am a 21 year old student from London and I tested HIV positive in March 2010. Growing up, I was always aware of how many lives HIV was claiming, so when I was told that I had tested positive earlier this year, I was horrified by what was to become of me. For a while I felt as though my life had ended, I was not aware of how far treatment had come along as I had never known anyone with HIV and believed I was just handed over a death sentence.

I was offered counselling with a health advisor in my local HIV clinic and little by little I started to accept my diagnosis and also believe that I still had a future. I was also lucky as my boyfriend (who is negative) was very supportive and was always there when I needed a shoulder to cry on. Since my diagnosis I have started university and started to build my life up again.

I also told my story to a woman's magazine company in the September issue with the goal of making people more aware of the risks of HIV and encouraging them to test, as from what I have now learnt, it is not a death sentence and you're better off knowing your status. I felt very proud when I received letters back from readers saying how my story had encouraged them to go and get tested and one of the readers who wrote back to the magazine about my story and how it had influenced her to get tested and do volunteer work won letter of the month.

HIV has changed my life dramatically, but I am glad I know my status as knowledge is power. My boyfriend of three years and I plan to remain together and have children once I have finished university. We practise safer sex 100% of the time from when I received my diagnosis.

As for stigma or discrimination, I cannot say that I have personally received any. My friend who I disclosed to and my partner have not treated me any differently to how they did before because I am still me. I'm glad that I have found such good support from doctors, nurses, health advisors, college counsellors and teachers, and friends which I have made from support groups such as Body and Soul and Positively UK (which I rang up quite frequently in the first few weeks of my diagnosis and they also phoned me to see how I was doing). Without their help I would not be as accepting of my illness as I am now.

Lily

Story from www.nat.org.uk/real-life-stories

Source 6 Lily's story

Getting it checked out

If you are at all concerned, or want to get anything checked out, there are all sorts of options available.

To start with, knowing where your local sexual health clinic is could be useful in the future. But there are also a wide range of free and confidential sexual health advice and contraception services for young people. They may be listed as: sexual health clinics, genitourinary medicine (GUM) clinics or family planning clinics. Brook is a national voluntary sector provider of free and confidential sexual health advice and services specifically for young people under 25.

Activity 4

Think back to what you have learned about condoms. Name three important things to remember to ensure condoms are used effectively.

5 Alcohol, tobacco and other drugs

5.1 Drugs – an introduction

By the end of 5.1 you will:
- be able to explain the word 'drug'
- be able to name different types of drugs
- be able to discuss what influences your perception of drug use and how this can differ from reality.

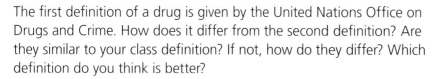

Starter

What does the word 'drug' mean? Discuss this question with a partner. Each pair will feed back to the class so that the class can agree upon a definition.

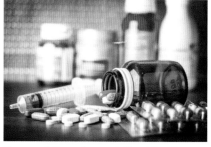

Source 1 How do we define 'drug'?

An international definition of the word 'drug' is: a substance people take to change the way they feel, think or behave.

Another possible definition is: a medicine or other substance which has a physiological effect when ingested or otherwise introduced into the body.

The first definition of a drug is given by the United Nations Office on Drugs and Crime. How does it differ from the second definition? Are they similar to your class definition? If not, how do they differ? Which definition do you think is better?

You now have a definition of the word 'drug', but what else do you know about drugs?

Activity 1

Get into groups of four to answer the following questions. Then feed back your answers to the rest of the class:
1. What forms could a drug come in?
2. In what ways do people take drugs?
3. Why do people take drugs?
4. What effects do drugs have? How might they change the way a person feels, thinks or behaves?
5. What legal substances are also drugs? Could medicines be included in this definition?
6. Are tobacco and alcohol also drugs? What is it about them that fits the United Nations' definition above?
7. Do gases, glues and solvents fit the United Nations' definition above? What is it about them that makes them a drug?

How do we classify drugs?

Activity 2

Copy the table in Source 2. With the help of a partner, try to sort the following drugs under the correct heading in the table.

Feed back to the class.

paracetamol	cigarettes	antihistamines
cocaine	cannabis	tranquilisers
anabolic steroids	Calpol	ecstasy
alcohol	antibiotics	synthetic cannabinoids
heroin	e-cigarettes	

Drugs which can be legally bought over the counter	Controlled drugs. These are prescribed drugs that are subject to strict legal controls	Drugs prescribed by a healthcare professional

Source 2 Drug types

You will find that some drugs can go under more than one heading. For example, antihistamines (usually taken for hayfever and allergies) can be bought over the counter but are also often prescribed. Some drugs, for example, alcohol and cigarettes, including e-cigarettes, are legal but have an age limit. Some prescription medicines are controlled under the Misuse of Drugs Act (and subsequent amendments). These medicines are called controlled medicines or **controlled drugs**.

Prescribed medicines are prescribed by a doctor or other health care professional. You must never take a drug that has been prescribed for someone else. When taking any drug, it is essential that you follow the instructions on the label. All drugs, including over-the-counter drugs and prescribed drugs, are dangerous if misused. It is therefore vital that all drugs are stored correctly, and out of reach of children.

Source 3 Some drugs, including e-cigarettes, are legal but have an age limit.

49

It is important to note that drug classifications are not necessarily based purely on potential harm.

Activity 3

Most psychoactive drugs fall into one of three drug types (although some have aspects from more than one): **depressants**, **stimulants** and **psychedelics**. Read the information in Source 4. Which type is each of the following drug?

- caffeine
- LSD
- alcohol
- cocaine
- nicotine

Stimulants *increase* the levels of certain chemicals (called neurotransmitters) in the central nervous system (CNS), including the brain. These tend to result in increased alertness and energy. These drugs also make your heart beat faster, increase blood pressure, and speed up your breathing, which cause more stress on your body.

Depressants *slow down* CNS activity. These tend to slow down your heart rate, lower your blood pressure, and slow down your breathing. The CNS depression also means users feel less pain and more relaxation, which is accompanied by reduced fine motor control (clumsiness). It is important to note that the term depressant only refers to the effect on the CNS, not on mood. Depressants tend to induce euphoria, rather than sadness, especially in moderate amounts.

Psychedelics are most commonly known for their hallucination-inducing properties. They are thought to increase and change connections within the brain which alters perception. Things like time, distance, and the self stop being prioritised in the mind, which can be dangerous if in a hazardous environment (e.g. chasing a beautiful butterfly on a road).

Source 4 Stimulants, depressants and psychedelics

Source 5 Is caffeine a stimulant, depressant, or psychedelic?

Activity 4

Many people have different ideas about drugs, and what they think may be influenced by the media.

Look at the headlines in Source 6 and use them to discuss the following questions:

1 Where do people get their ideas and information about drugs from?
2 What impressions do these headlines give you about drugs?
3 Do you think the information about drugs in newspapers and magazines, and on television and the internet is accurate? Give reasons.

Detectives investigating possible link to MDMA after teenage found unconscious in park

A fifth of young drug users admit to taking 'mystery white powders' without any idea what they contain

Figures show number of hard drug users is rising

Will testing drugs really make users safe?

Should drug addicted kids be forced into rehab?

County lines drugs blamed for Kent's big rise in knife crime

Source 6 Headlines

It is important to get the correct information about alcohol, tobacco and other drugs. Your teacher will not be an expert on drugs and will probably be learning about the names of some drugs and their effects, and the laws around drugs, at the same time as you. Learning together as a class, with your teacher, is a good way to explore what you need to know about drugs. For example, you will be learning about laws, the effects of drugs and where to go for help, advice and support.

Activity 5

Research local support groups where you can get help, advice and support about drugs.

5.2 Drugs and the law

By the end of 5.2 you will:
- be able to give some facts about the Misuse of Drugs Act 1971 (and subsequent amendments)
- be able to identify situations where people may be breaking the law.

Starter

Can you share any facts about drugs, and about drugs and the law, in particular? Discuss with a partner and be prepared to feed back to the class.

The likelihood is that you will know a lot about the dangers of drugs – but it's important to remember that some drugs can be very helpful.

When drugs are licensed to be used as medicines in this country, they have been through a series of trials to try to make sure they are as safe as possible.

You will now know that taking any drug, even medicines, can cause problems. For that reason, society gives careful thought to the way it allows drugs to be used.

The Misuse of Drugs Act classifies drugs into three groups: Class A, Class B and Class C. Each class carries different legal penalties for having the drugs or for selling them/giving them away.

Activity 1

Do you know any rules about drugs in your school? (Remember 'drugs' refers to all drugs including medicines, volatile substances/solvents, alcohol, tobacco and illegal drugs.)

In pairs, think of two rules. Why do you think the school introduced these rules? Be prepared to share this information with the class.

Activity 2

The photos in Source 2 show a variety of drugs that are controlled under the Misuse of Drugs Act. Working in pairs, discuss and then decide which class you think each drug belongs to in the table in Source 1. You may wish to look up some of the information at **www.spa.police.uk/forensic-services/drug-analysis/types-of-drugs/**

Class	Maximum penalty for possession (having them)	Maximum penalty for supplying (selling or giving them away)
A	Up to seven years in prison or an unlimited fine or both	Up to life in prison or an unlimited fine or both
B	Up to five years in prison or an unlimited fine or both	Up to fourteen years in prison or an unlimited fine or both
C	Up to two years in prison or an unlimited fine or both	Up to fourteen years in prison or an unlimited fine or both

Source 1 The Misuse of Drugs Act – maximum penalties

Amphetamines

Cannabis

Ecstasy

Heroin

LSD

Magic mushrooms

Tranquillisers

Khat

Cocaine

Synthetic cannabis

Ketamine

GHB

Crack cocaine

Source 2 Different drugs covered by the Misuse of Drugs Act

The Misuse of Drugs Act 1971 has been amended many times. This reflects attitudes towards certain drugs, developments in the world of medicine or the introduction of new substances. The Misuse of Drugs Act does not cover all drugs. The Medicines Act covers the use and supply of medicines and there are other laws that control the use and supply of alcohol, tobacco and solvents.

Activity 3

In each of the situations below is anyone breaking the law? If so, identify who is breaking the law and how.

Pat and Chris are fourteen. They are drinking cider on a street corner.

Pradip is sixteen. He goes into the local newsagent and buys cigarettes.

Danni is fifteen. She is with her friends in the shopping centre. She has some cannabis in her bag.

Aasif and Dayo are sitting in the park sniffing solvents.

Sam is at a party and gives Kim an ecstasy tablet which Kim accepts.

Alfie is eighteen. He is in a pub with his younger brother who is seventeen. He buys himself and his brother each a pint of beer.

'Legal highs'

Drugs formerly known as 'legal highs' are now called psychoactive drugs, and are covered by the 2016 Psychoactive Substances Act. This Act now covers all psychoactive substances (i.e. "any substance that is intended for human consumption that is capable of producing a psychoactive effect"). This also means that any new drugs are automatically illegal, except for certain products such as tobacco and alcohol, as well as controlled drugs (which remain under the Misuse of Drugs Act 1971). It's illegal to sell or give away drugs covered by the 2016 Psychoactive Substances Act. There's no penalty for possession (unless you're in prison). Supply and production can get you up to seven years in prison, an unlimited fine, or both.

However, in 2018, for the first time in the UK, expert doctors were given the option to legally issue prescriptions for cannabis-based medicines when they agree that their patients could benefit from this treatment.

Alcohol and the law

How old do I need to be to buy alcohol in the UK?

It is against the law for anyone under the age of 18 to buy alcohol – whether in a pub, shop, bar or club. It is also against the law for someone over the age of 18 to knowingly buy alcohol for someone under age – this is called buying by proxy. The person buying the alcohol for someone under 18 could face a fine and police caution.

What if I am out with the family, can I have a glass of cider with my dinner?

Basically, you cannot buy or be served alcohol if you are under 18 – the only exception is if you are with adults having a plated meal when you can have beer, wine or cider if the adults and owner of the establishment agree and if you are over 16. If this is in a pub you must be in an area set aside solely for eating meals.

But once I am 18, I can buy alcohol then?

Yes, but even if you are over 18 and you don't have ID, shopkeepers and licensed premises can refuse to serve you if you look younger.

What if the police catch me and my friends drinking in the park?

Police have the powers to confiscate alcohol from under 18s drinking in public spaces (for example, on the street or in parks).

What are the laws on drinking and driving?

It is against the law for an adult to drive with more than 50 mg of alcohol per 100 ml of their blood in Scotland (80 mg per 100 ml in England, Wales and Northern Ireland). If they break the law, they could face a fine of £5000, six months in prison and having their licence taken away for at least a year. Causing death through drink-driving can result in a maximum prison sentence of 14 years and a two-year driving ban. This also applies to a 17-year-old driver, although their age may be taken in to account when being sentenced.

Is the law the same throughout the world?

Most countries have a legal drinking age of at least 18 years old – in the USA it's 21! Drink drive laws are even stricter in most other countries and in some countries drinking alcohol at all before driving is against the law. Other countries have special low limits for young or inexperienced drivers.

Source 3 Alcohol and the law

Activity 4

It may be against the law for anyone, regardless of age, to drink alcohol in some public places. Do you know if your town or area has rules about this? What else do you know about alcohol and the law?

Does your town or area have rules about drinking alcohol in public places?

Activity 5

Laws and facts about drugs are quite complicated. There is a lot of misinformation and misunderstanding. Identify one new thing you have learned today. How could it help you and your friends?

By the end of 5.3 you will:
- know the recommended health advice regarding alcohol consumption for adults
- be able to explain the effects of drinking too much alcohol.

Starter

Think about some popular TV shows (for example, soap operas, dramas, reality TV). Which ones have the characters meeting up in pubs, bars and clubs? How realistic is this?

Some TV shows, soaps in particular, can be focused around a pub which can make regularly drinking alcohol seem like a normal part of everyday life! Even so, although underage alcohol use remains prevalent, surveys seem to show that young people may be becoming more aware of the harms of alcohol and getting slightly more conservative in their experimentation with it. Let's have a think about the effect that alcohol has on the body and some of the risks …

Activity 1

Look at Source 1 and discuss in pairs what effect you think drinking alcohol would have on the different parts of the body that are labelled. This is an adult's body. Remember that the same amount of alcohol would have a much bigger effect on a child or a young person.

Be prepared to feed back to the class.

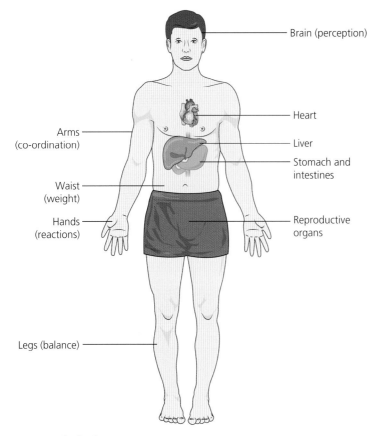

Brain (perception)

Heart

Arms (co-ordination)

Liver

Stomach and intestines

Waist (weight)

Hands (reactions)

Reproductive organs

Legs (balance)

Source 1 The body

Activity 2

Working on your own, design a meme that encourages adults to keep within the safe limit recommendations. The accompanying caption should give simple and direct facts about units of alcohol and what constitutes a 'safe' amount. Source 2 provides some information on roughly how many units are in different types of alcoholic drinks.

The NHS and UK Chief Medical Officers advise that adults should not drink more than 14 units a week. If they do drink as much as 14 units, this should be spread out over three days or more. Remember that this is guidance for people over 18 (and who are also healthy). There are times when adults shouldn't drink at all too, such as when planning to drive, when pregnant, when on certain medications, doing a responsible or dangerous job or sports, for example. If people drink more than the recommended amount, they are putting themselves at more risk of developing certain illnesses.

Small glass of wine = 1.5 units

Large glass of wine = 3 units

Single shot of spirits = 1 unit

Pint of beer or cider = 3 units

Bottle of beer or cider = 1.7 units

Can of beer or cider = 2 units

You can find the number of units in other drinks by visiting the drinkaware unit calculator www.drinkaware.co.uk/understand-your-drinking/unit-calculator. You can also compare drinking with that of others with this app: www.globaldrugsurvey.com/brand/drinks-meter/.

Source 2 Units in some common drinks – reproduced courtesy of *Drugs And Me*.

Activity 3

In groups of four, read the scenarios in Source 3 and answer the questions.

Activity 4

If you wanted to find out more information on alcohol for yourself, a friend or a member of your family, where would you go or who could you talk to?

The group always hung out together in the school holidays. This summer, one or two of them decided they wanted to see what getting drunk felt like. They didn't think they had drunk all that much but suddenly Joe passed out and collapsed on the floor. Nobody knew if it was the alcohol or if something else had gone wrong.

Joe

1 What advice would you give the group?

2 What should they do to help Joe?

3 What do you think they should say to Joe's parents?

4 What do you think they should say to their own parents?

Luci and Rob's dad drinks a lot of alcohol. He often gets very drunk. Sometimes it is so bad he doesn't get up to go to work. When he does go to work, he usually gets there late. Their mum is worried sick about the family and is scared that dad is going to lose his job. Both the children are worried and want to do something to make things better.

Luci and Rob

1 What advice would you give Luci and Rob?

2 How could they help their mum?

3 How could they find out where to get help?

4 If the children hadn't talked to each other about their worries, who else could they have talked to?

Source 3

By the end of 5.4 you will:

- understand the effects of nicotine, tar and carbon monoxide on the body
- understand how the components of cigarettes lead to disease
- be able to identify the benefits of quitting smoking and how to access support to do so.

Starter

Look at Source 1. Why have attitudes towards smoking changed?

Activity 1

Copy and complete the sentences below using the words from the word box.

carcinogen	brain	cigarettes	heart	stimulant
addicted	poisons	cancer	chemicals	Smokers
	longer	emphysema	bronchitis	oxygen

Smoking – what are the risks to health?

The ____ someone smokes for and the more they smoke, the higher the risk of developing lung ____.

Regular smokers can get infections in their lungs. One infection is called ____.

Another long term effect of smoking is ____, which makes getting enough oxygen into the blood very difficult.

The chemicals

There are thousands of different ____ in ____, some of them are ____.

Nicotine is a ____ which affects the ____: it is this that causes people to become ____ to cigarettes.

Tar is a ____, which means it is a poison that causes cancer.

Carbon monoxide stops blood cells being able to carry as much ____ around the body as they should which harms cells, including the ____ and blood vessels.

Smoking is associated with:

- cancer (for example, throat, lung or mouth cancer)
- emphysema
- heart disease
- asthma
- bronchitis
- heart failure
- blockages in the arteries.

Source 1 Attitudes towards smoking have changed. The top image is a cigarette advert from the 1960s. The bottom image is modern, and encourages people to stop.

Activity 2

Imagine you are a YouTuber and you have been asked by NHS (Scotland) to create a video leading up to 'Stoptober' about why young people shouldn't start smoking. What would be the key messages? Outline a plan for the video.

I was smoking around a pack a day for fifteen years when I decided to give up. I wanted to give up because I hated being dependent on cigarettes and it was becoming socially much more unacceptable to smoke. It was hard as I craved cigarettes all the time for around two months. At the start I avoided being around other smokers so there was no temptation! I then did the 'Stoptober' challenge and after that, it got much easier. Two years on, I love being smoke-free!

Source 2

10 self-help tips to stop smoking

1. Think positive. You might have tried to quit smoking before and not managed it, but don't let that put you off.
2. Make a plan to quit smoking. Make a promise, set a date and stick to it.
3. Consider your diet. Some foods, including cheese and vegetables, make cigarettes taste worse and therefore less appealing.
4. Change what you drink. Cigarettes are less satisfying when consumed with water or juice, as opposed to tea, coffee or fizzy drinks.
5. Identify when you crave cigarettes.
6. Get some stop smoking support.
7. Get moving. Even a five-minute walk or stretch cuts cravings and may help your brain produce anti-craving chemicals.
8. Make non-smoking friends.
9. Keep your hands and mouth busy.
10. Make a list of reasons to quit.

For more information, visit www.nhsinform.scot/healthy-living/stopping-smoking

Activity 3

Read Source 2. In pairs, answer the questions below. Be prepared to feed back to the class.
1   Why is it so hard to give up smoking?
2   What are the benefits of giving up?
3   What products are available to help people give up?
4   What has the government done to help people to stop smoking?

Source 3 How can you quit?

An electronic cigarette (e-cigarette) is a device that allows you to inhale nicotine without most of the harmful effects of smoking. E-cigarettes work by heating and creating a vapour from a solution that typically contains nicotine; a thick, colourless liquid called propylene glycol and/or glycerine; and flavourings. As there's no burning involved, there's no smoke. E-cigarettes do not produce tar and carbon monoxide, two of the main toxins in conventional cigarette smoke. Some smokers have successfully used e-cigarettes to help them give up smoking.

However, the vapour from e-cigarettes has been found to contain some potentially harmful chemicals also found in cigarette smoke, although at much lower levels. E-cigarettes are still fairly new and we will not have a full picture on their safety until they have been in use for many years.

There are three types of safety concerns associated with e-cigarettes:

■ a fault with the e-cigarette device that could make it unsafe to use

■ side effects to your health caused by using your e-cigarette

■ concerns over the chemicals in flavourants that are linked to lung cancer.

Activity 4

Think back to the Starter activity and how when cigarettes were first introduced, nobody really understood the dangers. Could the same be said about e-cigarettes today? Or should we welcome that they have helped some adults quit smoking?

Activity 5

What would you say to a younger friend or relative who was tempted to start smoking?

By the end of 5.5 you will:

- be able to explain the impact drugs have on society
- understand how drugs affect an individual's physical, mental and emotional health
- be able to say what addiction and dependency are.

Starter

When does drug use become a problem? Brainstorm ideas with the rest of the class.

Drug use can never be 100 per cent safe. Even legal drugs may have side effects, or people may be allergic to them, or accidentally overdose on them. Using illegal drugs has additional risks. Illegal drugs are not made in medically controlled conditions, so people cannot be sure what's in them. We read about drugs in newspapers and magazines, see them on TV and maybe even hear about them from friends. Some alcohol and other drug users stumble into misuse/harmful use. Often, we hear about drugs in relation to addiction. When you hear somebody described as a drug addict, what do you think of? Do you think the term 'drug addict' is helpful? Do you think someone can develop problematic drug use without displaying the typical 'tell-tale' signs you might expect?

Activity 1

If a person develops a substance use disorder, how might this impact their:

- health (mentally and physically)
- employment/finances
- family
- friends
- education
- travel
- freedom?

Smoking – the UK's single greatest cause of preventable illness and early death.

Drug addiction is characterised by compulsive drug-seeking.

The physical effects of smoking cannabis can result in bloodshot eyes, a dry mouth and very slow reflexes.

A person caught using cannabis may be arrested.

Teenagers may be especially prone to risky behaviour, including trying drugs.

Alcohol misuse can have a devastating effect on families, and is strongly linked to abuse and neglect.

Someone might take drugs to feel more confident.

Someone might live in an environment where their friends or family use drugs.

Source 1

Tobacco
Cost
£1.1 billion
Deaths each year
~10,000

Total cost
£8.2 billion
Total deaths
~12,323

Alcohol
Cost
£3.6 billion
Deaths each year
1,136 (2018)

Drugs misuse
Cost
£3.5 billion
Deaths each year
1,187 (2018)

Costs to society may come due to healthcare, social care, criminal justice, or loss to the economy

Source 2 Costs to Scottish society

Mental health

Drugs and mental health are linked in a few ways.

1 Using drugs (legally or illegally) or alcohol can be a way to deal with difficult emotions. This is known as self-medication. For some people it might help with the pain of mental health problems. Mental health problems that affect someone's judgement could also make them more likely to take drugs.

2 Sometimes people reach a point where they feel unable to cope without drugs. This is called addiction.

3 There's always a risk that drug use could make a mental health condition worse, or make someone more likely to develop a mental health problem. For example, there's a link between cannabis use and paranoia, while other drugs like LSD and magic mushrooms can produce psychosis.

Drugs and dependency

Tobacco and alcohol are the most commonly used drugs in the UK and a lot of people are dependent on them. Feeling the need to have another cigarette or drink to get through the day can make life difficult. That's why a lot of people try to stop, but it isn't easy for them to stop on their own. They need help and support.

Physical dependence can happen because of the long-term (chronic) use of many drugs, including prescription drugs, even if they are taken as instructed. Physical dependence does not necessarily mean someone is addicted, but it often accompanies addiction. This distinction can be difficult to see, particularly with prescribed pain medications. For example, if someone needs higher and higher doses, it can mean that they are developing a tolerance to the drug, or it may be that their problem or illness is getting worse. It does not necessarily mean the beginning of abuse or addiction.

If someone cannot stop using a drug, even though there are harmful consequences, and if they are failing to meet work, social and family obligations, it can be classified as an addiction. There can be a physical dependence where the body adapts to the drug and needs more of it to get a certain effect (tolerance). The person will have drug-specific physical or mental symptoms if the drug use is stopped suddenly (called withdrawal).

Activity 2

In pairs, look at Source 2.
1 Discuss the problems caused to society due to the costs of alcohol, tobacco and other drug misuse.
2 In what ways do you think that the people of Scotland would benefit from a reduction in these problems caused to society?
3 Research how Scotland compares with other countries around the world in terms of problems caused to society by alcohol, tobacco and other drugs.
4 Now feed back and discuss all your answers with the rest of your class.

Activity 3

People who help you learn about drugs often say, 'All medicines are drugs but not all drugs are medicines.' What is the important point that they are making?

Activity 4

1 Does someone who has an alcoholic drink before they go to bed have a substance use disorder? Are they dependent?
2 If someone takes a painkiller following surgery or injury but finds that they are still taking them a month later, what should they do?

Discuss these two questions in pairs. Be prepared to feed back to the class.

Activity 5

Reflect on what you have learned this learning opportunity. Give one reason to explain why talking about 'drug dependency' is more helpful than talking about 'drug addiction'.

By the end of 5.6 you will:

- be able to identify the impact of 'risk' taking with drugs
- know how to assess and manage risky situations involving drugs
- know that there is help and support available for people who have problems with drugs.

FRANK is the National Drugs Helpline: **0300 123 6600** If you want to talk, you can call FRANK free, 24 hours a day, 365 days a year.

What is 'risk'?

Risk is the chance that harm might be caused. When we think about risk we need to think about two things:

1 the *what* – the harms that might happen to us

2 the *might* – the likelihood that harm will happen to us.

Take, for example, the risk of a bungee rope snapping. The chance of being harmed if the rope snaps mid-jump is high, but the likelihood of this happening is low. Bungee jumping is highly regulated, there are many safety tests and, considering the number of jumps each day, the actual risk is 1 in 500 000 jumps being fatal. Some risks are part of everyday life.

Starter

What events can you think of where drugs being present could lead to risky situations occurring? Think of one example for each of the following:
- prescription medicines
- alcohol
- illegal drugs.

Bungee jumping

Parkour

Texting to ask someone out on a date

Speaking in front of your class

Source 1

Taking drugs is never risk free and different situations will present different levels of risk. Social situations may be risky because sometimes we leave it up to our friends to do the thinking for us.

Chantelle is invited with Surina and Rash to Jade's fourteenth birthday party. She thinks her parents might not approve but she is going to go anyway.

On the way to the party, Chantelle bumps into Mark, who she knows from school. He has some vodka. He suggests they stop in the park and have a pre-drink on the way to the party.

Surina and Rash are already at the party. They are dancing and having a good time.

Rash has some cigarettes. He offers one to Surina. She is not sure whether to take one but Rash says that he only smokes occasionally and can stop whenever he wants.

The party is in full swing. Chantelle thought that Jade's parents were going to be in but they are not. A big group of young people, who are older, arrive at the door, demanding to be let in. It appears that Jade created an event on social media which has been seen by a lot of people.

Chantelle has a bit too much to drink and feels sick. Surina helps her sit on the stairs to settle down a bit. Surina offers Chantelle coffee to sober her up.

Someone that Chantelle doesn't know has some cannabis. She offers some to Chantelle. She has never tried it before. She is not sure whether to try it or not.

Chantelle feels really unwell and so decides to walk home on her own. She leaves the party. She can't call home for a lift as she hasn't told her parents that she was going to the party.

Outside the party, she bumps in to a friend of her older brother's. He offers her a lift home.

Source 2 The party

Activity 1

Read the scenarios in Source 2. Work in pairs. Consider the risks posed in each individual scenario. Where would you put them on the ladder of risk? How could the risk be lessened in each case? Try to bring each risk down the ladder.

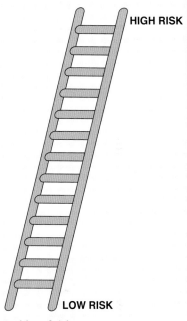

HIGH RISK

LOW RISK

Ladder of risk

Be prepared to feed back to the class once you have considered the risks posed in each scenario.

Activity 3

Imagine you could sit down with one of the characters in the scenarios in Source 2 and offer them a piece of good advice. What would it be?

Activity 2

Remember that there is support and advice available. Name some websites that you can visit for help on issues around drugs.

Activity 4

Now think about different drugs and why they might involve risks. Here are five statements designed to test your awareness on the topic of drugs and risks. Decide whether you think each statement is true or false.

1 Smoking only a few cigarettes a day is fine.
2 Alcohol slows down the brain.
3 Giving your own prescription medicines to someone else isn't a problem.
4 At least one young person a month dies from sniffing solvents.
5 You could be sent to prison for five years for being found with cannabis.

Despite all the information we have about drugs, people still take risks.

Different people have different reasons for taking risks with drugs.

Here are some of the reasons people give:

- curiosity
- for a dare
- because they like the feeling
- to show off

- boredom
- to help someone
- because they are influenced by someone else.

Source 3 Why do people still take risks?

Activity 5

The worst thing you can do in an emergency is nothing. Read Source 4, Keeley's story.

Why is it important to take action in an emergency? What are the important things to remember?

Rees is at a party. He sees a girl, who he later finds out is called Keeley, on the floor.

Rees sees Keeley collapsed on the floor.

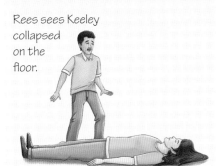

He checks for dangers and calls for help.

Reena arrives on the scene and dials 999.

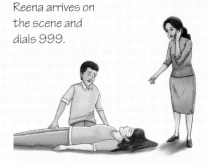

Rees checks whether Keeley is breathing.

Keeley is breathing so Rees puts her in the recovery position.

Rees checks that Reena has called the ambulance. Reena is looking out for it.

Rees checks Keeley's breathing again.

Keeley is not breathing so Rees starts to administer CPR.

The ambulance arrives.

Source 4 Keeley's story

Activity 6

Identify something new that you have learned in this learning opportunity about drugs and risk.

By the end of 6.1 you will:
- understand what 'emotional wellbeing' and 'mental health' are.

Starter

It's often easier to recognise someone's physical wellbeing than their emotional wellbeing. Often people find it more comfortable to talk about physical health but may find talking about emotional wellbeing more of a challenge.

In pairs, discuss what contributes positively to your emotional wellbeing. Source 1 might give you some inspiration! Be prepared to feed back to the class.

Emotional wellbeing means how you are feeling at the moment and how you cope with everyday life. Emotional wellbeing can change all the time.

Mental health is defined as: how a person thinks, feels, and behaves or reacts. Our mental health determines how effectively we respond to challenges, to stress, or relate to other people, make choices, or function successfully in our community.

We can learn to develop and improve our wellbeing and mental health.

Source 1 What makes us feel good?

Good mental health is a sense of positive emotional wellbeing, confidence and self-esteem. It helps us to fully enjoy and appreciate other people, day-to-day life and our environment. When we are mentally healthy, we can:

- form positive relationships
- use our abilities to reach our potential
- cope with life's challenges
- contribute positively to our communities.

A person's mental health and emotional wellbeing will change, depending on what is happening in their life. Events can affect everyone in different ways, and it is important to remember that all experiences can have an impact on our mental health.

Activity 1

In pairs, come up with a list of situations that might affect someone's mental health and emotional wellbeing.

What does 'mental health' mean? The charity Mind explains it like this:

> In many ways, mental health is just like physical health: everybody has it and we need to take care of it.
>
> Good mental health means being generally able to think, feel and react in the ways that you need and want to live your life. But if you go through a period of poor mental health you might find the ways you're frequently thinking, feeling or reacting become difficult, or even impossible, to cope with. This can feel just as bad as a physical illness, or even worse.

According to the SCSC (Scottish Children's Services Coalition):

- around one in ten of 5–16 years olds in Scotland have a clinically diagnosable mental health problem

- one in five of young adults (teenagers) in Scotland may experience a mental health problem in any given year.

Whether it is family or friends, neighbours or school/work colleagues, the chances are we know someone who is affected. This figure is only a snapshot in time. Many argue that mental health problems are actually more widespread than this.

There's a big range of things that people might experience when their mental health is under pressure. For example, a person might feel very sad and want to cry, or perhaps think it's not worth getting out of bed in the morning. These feelings are perfectly natural and do not necessarily mean that someone is experiencing mental health problems – but if those things continue, and build up, then there might be a problem, such as depression or anxiety. If you do need some support, never hesitate to ask for it, whether it is from an adult you trust, a teacher, your doctor, or from mental health support groups. Look at Source 1 in 6.8 for some contacts that you could use.

Getting It Right For Every Child (**GIRFEC**) is a **national approach in Scotland**. Its target is to support children and young people so that they can grow up feeling loved, safe, respected, and able to realise their full potential. At home, in school or the wider community, every child and young person should be:

Safe

Healthy

Achieving

Nurtured

Active

Respected

Responsible

Included

Those words are known as SHANARRI.

Source 2 SHANARRI

Activity 2

In groups of 3 or 4 look at Source 2 and the SHANARRI words in it, then:
1 Work out what each word means. You will be asked to feedback to your class. Update your answers if you hear better ones.
2 For each of the SHANARRI words decide why it is important for every child and young person to be like that (e.g. be safe) for their mental health and wellbeing.

Activity 3

Sometimes things build up inside us so much that we think we might explode! Imagine blowing air into a balloon until that point where the air pressure inside is so great that the balloon can't take any more. You can let the air out of a balloon to reduce the pressure. What can a person do to reduce the pressure on them and let their feelings out? Work in pairs to come up with some examples.

Activity 4

How easy do you think it would be for someone in your school who was feeling down to be able to say so and ask for help? Give some reasons to explain your answer.

Activity 5

In groups, discuss and come up with other examples of the way poor mental health might show itself in people.

By the end of 6.2 you will:
- identify what affects your confidence and self-esteem
- be able to describe how resilience can help you.

Resilience

A definition of resilience could be: a set of qualities that helps a person cope with the negative feelings that happen when they are experiencing difficult life events

There are two ways to balance the times when we are negative about ourselves. The first is to think about positive ways to describe ourselves. The second is being honest about our positive qualities – don't be too shy to say when you are good at something.

The game in Activity 1 relies on you being honest and positive.

Activity 1

Your teacher will give you some cards. Place the pile upside down in the centre of your group. Listen carefully to the instructions on how to play the game. You are free to pass *once* if you can't think how to complete the sentence on the card or you may ask other group members to help you.

If you have a positive attitude you are more likely to feel better about yourself and about life in general. This is one way to be resilient. Look at Source 1. It shows two statements that somebody could have made about the same situation.

Source 1 Resilience

Starter

Young people often find it really easy to list all their faults and failings, but they sometimes find it difficult to see their good points. Working in pairs, take turns to tell your partner one thing about yourself that is good or positive.

Activity 2

The sayings in Source 2 are great for helping an individual to become more resilient and get a positive outlook on life. However, sometimes a whole group can become negative. Some members of a group can sometimes impact on the way others view things, even when they don't mean to.

As a class, discuss and come up with some mottos or sayings that could help your class stay positive.

Another way of being resilient is to use sayings to help you see the positive side of life. Look at Source 2.

> 'Persistence and resilience only come from having been given the chance to work through difficult problems.'
>
> *Gever Tulley*
>
> 'Do not judge me by my success, judge me by how many times I fell down and got back up again.'
>
> *Nelson Mandela*

Source 2 Resilience sayings

Taking an exam

When things go wrong I ...	Not great	OK	Good	Excellent
take responsibility for my actions		✔		
am skilled at solving my own problems			✔	
stay positive and optimistic	✔			
am able to talk about it and seek help			✔	

Source 3 How resilient am I?

If you do need some support, never hesitate to ask for it, whether it is from an adult you trust, a teacher, your doctor, or from mental health support groups. Look at Source 1 in 6.8 for some contacts that you could use.

Activity 3

Why is it that some people seem to bounce back after being hit by life's problems, while others find it more difficult? Think back to some of the big challenges in your life: your first day at school; making friends; your performance for the sports team; your role in the Christmas pantomime; sitting tests and exams; moving up to secondary school. We've all faced challenges in some or all of these areas. Think of some of the things you have learned that would tell your 'past self' that would have helped you to be more resilient. Will this advice also help you in the future?

Activity 4

Look at the example in Source 3. It shows how one person rates their own resilience. For example, they think they are not good at staying positive and optimistic but they do feel able to talk and seek help. Construct your own chart or table which helps you recognise how resilient you are. Next, with a partner, help to suggest ways to improve each others' resilience.

By the end of 6.3 you will:

- be able to share a range of strategies for boosting emotional resilience.

Starter

As we know, people's mental health and emotional wellbeing can change in response to what is happening in their life. People can react differently to different events – and we might find that people seem more resilient at different times. In pairs, discuss what it means to be 'resilient'. Think of some examples of resilience. Be prepared to feed back to the class.

Another way of explaining what 'resilience' means is by saying 'it is how well we cope'. We can boost our resilience and improve our own ability to cope with difficult feelings and problems. We can make ourselves resilient people who:

- focus on changing the things in our lives within our control
- have goals and want to achieve them
- cope well with what happens in our lives and believe that the future is bright
- don't worry about what other people think of us, enjoy healthy relationships, and who don't allow our peers to pressure us into doing anything we don't want to do.

Connect

Stay in touch with loved ones. This helps us to feel more secure and happy. Having a chat can lift our mood.

Be active

This is good for both physical health and mental health and wellbeing

Take notice

Take time to be aware of the world around you. How are others feeling, what the is world like at that moment. Enjoy that moment.

Learn

Learning improves your self-esteem (how you feel about yourself). It may also give you a chance to meet new people.

Give

People who display an interest in helping others are more likely to see themselves as happy. Try volunteering.

Source 1 Five ways to better wellbeing

Activity 1

Source 1 shows five ways to better wellbeing. You can find these at Mind (www.mind.org. uk/workplace/mental-health-at-work/taking-care-of-yourself/five-ways-to-wellbeing/) with some extra suggestions on what you could do.

Read over the five suggestions and, in pairs or small groups, make a list of things you could do individually or with your family for each of the five suggestions that could help to improve your and your family's wellbeing.

Activity 2

Can you think of a time when someone has seemed very resilient? They can be people you know or people you have read or heard about.

Activity 3

If you were to develop one new coping strategy that would help you to build up your resilience, what would it be?

Joe's story

Joe had been off school for quite a while because he had to have an operation. While he was at home recovering, the family received some sad news – his grandma, who lived abroad, had died. Joe was sad that he would not see her again and knew that both his parents were really upset as well.

When he got back to school he was disappointed to find that his doctor wouldn't let him take part in any PE learning opportunities – and even worse he couldn't play football so that meant he was no longer part of the school team.

To cap it all, Mark, his best friend, announced he would be moving away at the end of term because his mother had a new job in another town.

Joe began to feel really depressed. He didn't look forward to going to school and he felt sad when he was at home. It seemed that everything he was used to was changing. His friends noticed he was becoming very quiet and keeping to himself.

It is important to address problems before they become too big to manage. Sometimes it is helpful to break a problem down in to manageable chunks: this often helps when tackling school work, revision and homework. Sharing a problem with friends to get their thoughts and ideas often helps. Turning a 'problem' into a 'challenge' can make us view a problem differently – looking at it as something to overcome and not something to stop us moving forward.

This is a step-by-step approach to dealing with a problem:

1 Identify a problem in your life.

2 Share ideas of ways to tackle the problem, brainstorming with others if possible.

3 Show an awareness of how challenges and obstacles can present opportunities to grow and develop.

If you do need some support, never hesitate to ask for it, whether it is from an adult you trust, a teacher, your doctor, or from mental health support groups. Look at Source 1 in 6.8 for some contacts that you could use.

Activity 4

Look at the list in Source 2 and discuss why each item might help someone maintain their emotional wellbeing.

Can you think of anything else that helps look after emotional wellbeing? Make a list of your ideas.

- Remember times when you felt safe and looked after.
- Make sure you get enough sleep.
- Try to eat healthily.
- Get enough exercise you enjoy, for example swimming, cycling, running.
- Spend time caring for something or someone else, for example looking after a pet, or helping a neighbour.
- Talk to someone you feel close to.
- Spend time with good friends who are helpful and look out for you.

Source 2 Looking after yourself

Activity 5

Hashtags are often used in social media to group thoughts and ideas, so that people can search for a particular topic more easily. Write a message about self care which includes one of these hashtags:
- #GetOutside
- #HappyNewDay
- #MondayMotivation
- #FeelingGood
- #EatWell

By the end of 6.4 you will:

- identify a range of strong emotions that affect how we feel
- understand how people can overcome negative feelings.

Fraser is fourteen years old and lives with his mum. This morning at breakfast she checked he'd done all his homework because recently he'd been late with several assignments. His mum soon realised that Fraser had not completed his maths homework. She was absolutely furious. Fraser had never heard her shout so much. She made him sit down and do it at the breakfast table.

Fraser left for school and asked his best friend Simon if he could see his homework. Simon said, 'No, you're always borrowing it.' At school he saw Amber and asked her the same question. Amber showed him her homework and they compared their answers, which were virtually the same.

Fraser and Amber made their way to the maths lesson and found a supply teacher standing in the room – their usual teacher was off sick.

Source 1 Fraser's story

If a relationship is important to us it can make us feel lots of strong emotions – both positive and negative. In Fraser's case while he knows his mum really loves him, he felt very hurt and upset when she lost her temper with him. These strong feelings apply whether the relationship is within your family or with friends: when someone is important to you, feelings matter.

happy jealous excited

worried ANTICIPATORY embarrassed

reassured spiteful APPRECIATED

loved faithful relaxed loyal

respected impressed

sociable fantastic outraged

TRUSTED threatened PRESSURED

RIDICULED reliable Unwanted

criticised irrepressible irritated

competitive ignored carefree

Source 2 Feelings

Although we all experience a range of emotions, it does sometimes feel as if they are happening to us and we are not in control of our feelings. When this happens, we can try to focus on positive ways to help improve our wellbeing.

This can be quite hard to do but we can work to develop the skills to use and improve the control we have over our lives.

Activity 3

Lucy and Carla were good friends. Lucy came out of Maths to see Carla whispering in the corridor with Seb and Mason. When Lucy approached them, they stopped talking. Lucy felt hurt. She turned away and stormed off towards the canteen. She didn't talk to Carla for the rest of the day. She felt really miserable and lonely. Carla tried to talk to Lucy but she wouldn't listen, she just kept turning her head away.

1 Why did Lucy feel hurt? What emotions was she experiencing?
2 Could she have taken another course of action rather than storming off and then ignoring Carla?

Lucy continued to ignore Carla at school the following day. She didn't answer any of Carla's messages. The anger built up inside Lucy. Every time someone spoke to Lucy, she snapped at them.

3 Did Lucy have a chance to sort this out? What could she have done?
4 How would Lucy have been feeling by the end of the day?

That evening when Lucy got home, she threw her schoolbag on the floor, pushed past her Mum and ran upstairs! It was her birthday and she was so unhappy. Carla, Seb and Mason were all sitting in the kitchen with Lucy's surprise birthday cake!

Lucy had jumped to conclusions and allowed negative feelings to take over. She was jealous and she over-reacted. She should have trusted her friend. If she had spoken to Carla rather than storming off, she may not have known the surprise that they were planning, but she would have realised that there was nothing to worry about. The lack of communication here made the problem worse.

Negative feelings:	Could have been managed with:
anger	trust
jealousy	open communication
sadness	keeping an open mind

'Flight, fright or freeze'?

Thousands of years ago, humans lived with constant threat of attack from members of other tribes or from wild animals. Our body's response to attack is called the 'flight, fright or freeze' and it is automatic. When our 'flight, fright or freeze' response is triggered, it causes lots of very quick changes in the body, by releasing hormones such as adrenaline. This makes our heart beat faster and our breathing to increase, so we can act. These are signs of anxiety. When we start to relax again, other hormones are released, and that can make us shake or feel unwell. We may feel faint or dizzy and this can make us panic.

Stress is not always bad. In small amounts it can be helpful. It can help us to carry out daily challenges, motivate us, and help us to complete tasks well. Too much stress, however, can have negative effects on us.

Stress is a response to something we feel is threatening while **anxiety** is a negative reaction to stress.

Feelings of anxiety are a natural response to stressful or dangerous situations. But for someone who experiences any kind of anxiety disorder, these feelings of anxiety, stress and panic can occur regularly and at any time, often for no apparent reason. If someone is having a panic attack, advise them to:

- not fight it and stay where they are, if possible
- breathe slowly and deeply (counting slowly)
- remember that the attack will pass
- focus on positive, peaceful and relaxing images
- remember they're safe and they have your support.

If you do need some support, never hesitate to ask for it, whether it is from an adult you trust, a teacher, your doctor, or from mental health support groups. Look at Source 1 in 6.8 for some contacts that you could use.

Activity 4

Practise a breathing technique you could use when you find yourself getting upset and angry.

By the end of 6.5 you will:
- understand the effects of negative relationships on emotional wellbeing
- understand the impact of 'body image' on emotional wellbeing.

In pairs, think about some of the things that might upset, worry or stress young people. Be prepared to feed back to the class.

Family should mean that arguments can be forgotten
Family should be there when you're feeling downtrodden...
...Unfortunately families, like most ideals, are never truly perfected
But this brute fact is not a curse but a blessing
We need our families to be imperfect, that we may experience but a small part of the conflict the world bears
So families need not be any of these things, all they need be ...
... Is Family

Source 1 An extract from 'It's All Relative' by Patrick Tolan

Family life and relationships

A 'family' might have one parent, or two mothers, or two fathers. There could be step-parents. Or you might not live with your parents but with adults who care for you.

Experiencing ups and downs in family life is normal. However, if you are having any problems at home that you're finding difficult, you can find information and support at places like Childline (**www.childline.org.uk/**). And if you are ever worried about abuse in your family or someone else's family you should talk to another adult or one of your teachers about this. You can read more and find further help at: **www.thehideout.org.uk**.

For some people, problems become too complicated for them to deal with on their own. Their best move is to tell a teacher or some other adult they like and trust.

Activity 1

Read Source 1. Everyone probably wishes they had the 'perfect family', but the poet in Source 1 recognises that there is no such thing as perfection where families are concerned. What things happen in reality that can cause problems in family life?

Activity 2

What strategies could you suggest to the young person in Source 2 to help them cope with what is going on?

Source 2 When it all gets too much

Sometimes relationships between the adults in a family break down so much that they decide to split up. This can have a really big impact on the young person. Even if they are used to hearing their parents rowing or seeing them ignoring each other, it still comes as a big shock.

The young person may feel totally confused, or it could be a relief if their parents' relationship had been very unhappy. Whatever the cause of the break-up, it is not the young person's fault. They did not cause it and they cannot mend it.

Alex and Ellie have been good friends for over a year. Alex notices that Ellie doesn't seem herself and often distracted when they are together. Sometimes Ellie shouts at Alex and calls him names. Alex is worried that Ellie doesn't want to be friends anymore. Alex is worried and sad and wants to talk about his feelings, but he is worried that this might make things worse. Alex knows Ellie's parents are splitting up and wonders if that is why Ellie is behaving this way.

Source 3

Activity 3

Read Source 3.

What advice can you give Alex? Write a script where Alex starts a conversation with Ellie. Try to find words that express Alex's feelings.

Body image

'Body image' is the mental picture you have of how you look, but it may or may not be similar to how others see you. If your emotional wellbeing stays low for a long time, you may be more at risk of experiencing a mental problem in the future, like depression, anxiety or an eating disorder. Comparing the way we look to others online, and in real life, and particularly on social media, may make us feel that we want to change the way we look. But it is important to remember that the images people post online, whether these are images of celebrities or of friends, show how they want others to see them and not always how they look in real life! You don't need a 'perfect' body to have a good body image.

When you don't like your body, the negative feelings can affect your emotional wellbeing. This can lead to anxiety and depression, and can show itself with the onset of eating disorders. If you are concerned about your body image, tell someone you trust what you are going through. Charities like Childline have pages dedicated to body image.

Activity 4

When talking about how people look and feel, the expression 'body image' is often used. But what does 'body image' really mean?

Work in pairs to come up with some ideas of what 'body image' means. Then list as many things as possible which affect our body image.

Drugs

Drugs and alcohol can impact on our mental health. They affect the way we see things, our mood and our behaviour.

For some people, taking drugs can lead to long-term mental health problems, such as depression or schizophrenia. Sometimes it is mental health issues that lead people to use drugs or turn to alcohol to cope. But then the drugs or the alcohol can often make them feel worse or lead to dependency. And if they are taking illegal drugs, they cannot be sure what they are taking and how their body and mind will react.

Wider world issues

We are regularly faced with information about serious issues around the world, online, on television, even in classes. These can make us anxious about how, or if, they will affect us. If your ability to cope with everyday life is harmed because of your anxiety you should try to find some helpful support.

If you do need some support, never hesitate to ask for it, whether it is from an adult you trust, a teacher, your doctor, or from mental health support groups. Look at Source 1 in 6.8 for some contacts that you could use.

Activity 5

We are told about wider world issues 24 hours a day, and they can become part of learning opportunities or of our lives.
1 In small groups identify recent wider world issues that could have or do create anxiousness for people.
2 What advice would you give to someone who is very anxious over issues such as these?

Activity 6

This learning opportunity began with a poem. Write your own three-line poem (it can be a haiku) about maintaining emotional wellbeing. Think about resilience and how to keep a positive outlook – even if things don't appear to be going well!

By the end of 6.6 you will:
- **understand how change can affect you**
- **identify some coping strategies and ways to access support.**

Most of us feel comfortable with things that we are used to, a 'sameness' in our lives. We get used to places, people, family, friends, structure, routines, opportunities, and even freedoms. We get used to how these things work and how we cope with or use them. We become comfortable. When change comes along it can knock us off our stride; things that were certain are not anymore.

We may experience differing intensities of reaction to different types of change. At the same time, not everyone will have the same reaction as you do to an identical problem.

Even changing to something that is much better can make us a bit nervous or anxious just because it is different.

They are going to build on the sports field. That's where I meet my friends and have the best times. I feel bad about that.

We are moving house. It's lovely but I worry that I won't see my friends again.

I have to move to another school. I feel anxious as I won't know people there or if I'll be as clever as them.

I used to get a lift to school but now have to make my own way there. I'm a bit nervous about doing it.

My sister is moving out to live in her own home. I'll miss her and I don't know when I'll see her.

I'm being moved to a different maths section. Will I cope with the work? Will the teacher like me? Will I have friends?

I've not been at school for quite a long time. I'm anxious about what it will be like to go back.

My new brother has just been born. I worry that I won't be loved as much. Will the baby make things difficult for me?

My dog died and I miss him so much. He was part of my family and I loved him. I feel so sad and upset.

My best friend is seeing other people more because she gets a different bus to school. Will she stop being my friend?

Source 1 Different types of changes

You might have experienced a range of different types of relationships in your life: a best friend or friends; a very close group of friends that you hang out with; long-standing friends from aspects of your life not connected with school; perhaps a boyfriend or girlfriend.

Sometimes relationships break down or end suddenly. When this happens, you may experience this change as loss. This could result in you feeling sad, less valued, rejected, lonely, embarrassed, or that you cannot trust other people.

Starter

In earlier chapters, we looked at change when you moved from primary to secondary school level and what caused you concerns before you moved up. This was a time of change. Work with a partner and discuss how moving from primary to secondary level was for each of you. Were you looking forward to it? Did you worry about it? What did you think would happen? What things were easier than you thought? What things are better than you thought? On your own, decide whether you think you and your partner worried about the same things, or if they worried more or less than you.

Activity 1

Look over Source 1. Pick out the changes that are similar to ones you have faced. For the ones chosen, think about how you reacted to them. What advice would you give to help someone who is going through the same types of changes? Be prepared to share your advice with the class.

Freddie's feelings

I'm going to be 15 next term. Three months ago Danielle, who I'd been going out with for over a year, suddenly said she was ending our relationship. She didn't give a reason, she just wanted out. The trouble is, I just can't seem to get over her. I think of Danielle all the time and keep remembering all the great time we had together. I can't believe how much it hurts – I still keep bursting into tears. I don't think I'll ever be able to trust anyone ever again

Anya's feelings

I'm 13 and play street hockey with my local youth club. We've been doing really well and I made it on to the team that is touring some Dutch youth clubs this summer. It's a great team and I was really looking forward to the tour. Now it's all gone wrong! I broke my ankle at the weekend and I'm going to have to be replaced on the tour. I'm totally fed up. I know the team will have a brilliant time and I won't be part of it. By the time they get back, I won't really be part of their group anymore. I'm feeling like an outsider already and I don't think I even want to go and see them off.

Source 2 Feelings

Some changes are hard to deal with. They may be in your family, your community, or at school. Try to create a 'coping kit' for yourself that you can turn to in times of anxiety or loss.

■ Why not start out with a simple breathing exercise that gives you the time to slow down all those worrying thoughts and gives you time to re-focus? Try this one. Breathe in through your nose for four seconds (put the tip of your tongue on the ridge at the top of your mouth behind your front teeth and this will help you to do this). Hold your breath for seven seconds (taking your tongue down slowly from the top of your mouth) and then slowly breathe out through your mouth for eight seconds trying to empty out all the air that you breathed in. This is a gentle exercise, do it softly. Repeat this exercise for five minutes.

■ If you can, lie down or sit and think about your body from its top to its toe. Work your way down, moving and relaxing everything until you reach the end of your toes. Once you have made your body relaxed, stay for a few minutes enjoying how relaxed your body is. You could even try your breathing exercise.

■ Write down your worries and take the time to get them organised. This should help you to understand your feelings better. It may help you to see solutions or to work out what you will need to get advice or support about.

■ Try using a stress ball, a ball that fits in your hand, that you can squeeze when you feel anxious.

Take time to build up your 'coping kit'. You could search the internet; there are lots of helpful sites. Try typing this into the search bar: 'relaxation methods for teens'.

Through life we will all face changes; some we deal with easily and others we may struggle with. Changes through loss, for example family members, family friends, pets, and school friends, can be very difficult emotionally and mentally. Our own 'coping kit' may help but it might not always be enough.

If you do need some support, never hesitate about asking for it, whether it is from an adult you trust, a teacher, your doctor, or from mental health support groups. Look at Source 1 in 6.8 for some of contacts that you could use.

Activity 2

Read about how Anya and Freddie are feeling in Source 2. In pairs, choose one of them to respond to with ideas that could help them to cope with their feelings of loss

Activity 3

Sit in your seat. Relax your body so that you feel comfortable. Try out our breathing exercise for a few minutes. While doing this you might like to think about somewhere that makes you feel calm, safe, comfortable, and happy.

Activity 4

In pairs or small groups, think about these questions:
1 What support is available in your school for someone who is struggling with change or loss?
2 Is there any support in the community that someone of your age could use in these situations?

By the end of 6.7 you will:

- be able to recognise some signs of common mental health problems, like anxiety and depression.

'I'm so depressed!' said Chiara, 'I didn't get into the netball team!'
Is Chiara genuinely depressed? Work in pairs to answer this question.
Be prepared to feed back to the class.

These are some of the psychological signs of depression:

- continuous low mood or sadness
- feeling hopeless and helpless
- having low self-esteem
- feeling tearful
- feeling guilt-ridden
- feeling irritable and intolerant of others
- having no motivation or interest in things
- finding it difficult to make decisions
- not getting any enjoyment out of life
- having suicidal thoughts or thoughts of self-harming
- feeling anxious or worried.

Mental health problems, like physical health problems, can affect different people in different ways. If you notice that someone is not taking an interest in their school work when they usually do, or are avoiding their friends or neglecting their hobbies or interests, and this has been going on for a while, then it could be a sign that they're struggling with their mental health.

Activity 1

What is depression? Which of these are physical signs of depression?

no energy   changes in appetite   changes in menstrual cycle
crying at a sad film   waking up tired   disrupted sleep
unexplained aches and pains   a growth spurt

Work with a partner and decide which of these can be physical signs of depression. Feed back to the class.

Activity 2

Read the scenarios in Source 1. In pairs, discuss the possible signs of someone struggling with their mental health, if any, in each case. Be prepared to feed back to the class.

Cameron knocks on Grace's door on the way to school. Grace hasn't been to school all week so Cameron wanted to check she is OK. Grace's Mum answers the door. She says that Grace won't be coming to school today as she is too tired. Grace's Mum says she's worried about her. She says she doesn't understand why she is so tired as she spends all her time in bed! She says that Grace just doesn't want to do anything at all. Grace's Mum has tried to get her to come downstairs for dinner but she says she is not hungry. Cameron sends Grace a message and says that everyone in class is missing her and he hopes she'll be back soon. Later that day, Grace replies saying that she doesn't ever want to come back to school.

'I just can't seem to snap out of it!' says Joe on the phone to his best friend, Adam. 'It all started when Dad got ill and I was really worried about him.' Adam tries to persuade Joe to meet him at the park, to chat about it. 'I just can't face anyone at the moment. Dad is better now and back at work, but I can't be bothered with anything anymore.'

Lucy has been up since 5 a.m. She can't sleep. She has an exam this morning and she is not sure if she has done enough revision. She always gets like this before exams. She is really nervous. She gets to school early and goes to the library to wait for her friends, before going to Breakfast Club.

Source 1

It can be completely normal to feel anxious and everyone will experience anxiety at different points in their life. This can be for many reasons; for example, they might have an exam or they might have to stand up and speak in public. However, anxiety can be hard to control for some people and it can have a big impact on their life.

They might:

- often feel restless or worried
- have trouble concentrating or sleeping
- experience dizziness or heart palpitations.

If you do need some support, never hesitate to ask for it, whether it is from an adult you trust, a teacher, your doctor, or from mental health support groups. Look at Source 1 in 6.8 for some contacts that you could use.

Breathing Space 0800 83 85 87 (www.breathingspace.scot)
Childline 0800 1111 (www.childline.org.uk)

Activity 3

Mental health problems are common. Yet most people still find it hard to speak openly about it. Design a poster bringing attention to 'Anxiety and Depression'. List some of the signs to look out for.

By the end of 6.8 you will:

- be able to advise others on how and when to get help in dealing with emotional wellbeing and mental health concerns.

Sometimes we cannot cope with problems on our own: we need help from other people. You don't need to try to cope on your own or wait for things to get worse. If you are worried, cross or sad, then talk to someone you trust. In pairs, make a list of adults that you could go to for help and support. Be prepared to feed back to the class.

Who can I turn to?

Don't do nothing. We all need to help make our mental health the best it can be and if that means talking to an adult, a teacher, or contacting a doctor or a support service, that's great.

And don't forget others; if you have to speak to someone to get them help, do it. If you can give them the names of people, organisations, internet sites or phone numbers to help support them, that's also great.

Be there for each other. Your support could be the difference.

When you have a problem or you are feeling low, you may turn to a close friend or a family member. As well as this though, it is also important to know who to go to in school. Your teacher will run through what support your school has in place with you.

Alternatively, you may wish to speak to someone that you don't know. You can call Childline free on 0800 1111 to talk confidentially to a counsellor.

You can also call the Samaritans on 116 123.

Activity 1

Look at the Childline website www.childline.org.uk and the range of practical resources it offers for children and young people. They are there to help them manage overwhelming emotions and feelings of sadness.

YoungMinds Crisis Messenger

Text message service for young people looking for help and support with mental health.

24 hours a day, 7 days a week.

Text: YM to 85258

www.youngminds.org.uk

NHS 24

Urgent health advice out of hours

Phone: 111

Shout

Text service if you are struggling to cope and need immediate help.

24 hours a day, 7 days a week.

Text: SHOUT to 85258

www.giveusashout.org

Childline

Support for anyone under 19 years old.

Phone: 0800 1111

www.childline.org.uk

NSPCC

Parent and child mental health support.

Phone: 0808 800 5000

Email: help@nspcc.org.uk

www.nspcc.org.uk

What else can I try?

As well as speaking to family, friends, or your school, or calling Childline or Samaritans, there are some other places you can go:

Look at Source 1. It gives you a list of contacts for you if you are concerned about your or someone else's mental health. Some of these services are open all the time but others have set hours when they can answer. If you are having a difficult time, keep trying until you get one that responds. There is always someone out there for you.

If you speak to an adult who you trust at home or at school, they may advise that you visit your local doctor or Youth Counselling Service. They can help you find the address and telephone number for contact, or you can look it up on the internet.

Activity 2

You are going to make a 'Who can help me?' flyer. Draw a circle in the middle of the sheet and draw yourself inside the circle. Write your name under your picture. Divide the page into two by drawing a line from the circle to each of the sides. Then divide each half in to three segments, as shown in Source 2:

In each segment write who can help and support you when you are feeling down.

Samaritans

Emotional support to anyone in emotional distress or at risk of suicide.

Open 24 hours a day, 365 days a year.

Phone: 116 123

Email: "mailto:jo@samaritans.org" jo@samaritans.org

www.samaritans.org

Cruse Bereavement Care

Helpline for those dealing with the loss of a loved one.

Phone: 0808 808 1677

Email: helpline@cruse.org.uk

www.cruse.org.uk

PAPYRUS

Young suicide prevention society.

Phone: 0800 068 4141

www.papyrus-uk.org

Source 1 Some support services

Friends	Family	School
	Me	
Call	Click	Visit

Source 2 Who can help me?

By the end of 7.1 you will:

- be able to say what 'being healthy' means
- be able to explain the importance of healthy routines in life.

Starter

What does 'being healthy' mean? If you were going to find out if someone was a healthy person, what kind of questions would you ask them?

Ten Ways to Stop Spreading Infections

✓ 1. Wash hands regularly and before touching food

✓ 2. Use a handkerchief/tissue when coughing or sneezing

✓ 3. Make sure used tissues go in a waste bin

✓ 4. Don't share combs or hairbrushes

✓ 5. Cover cuts with a dressing/plaster

✓ 6. Have vaccinations

✓ 7. Shower or bath regularly

✓ 8. Don't pick scabs or spots

✓ 9. Wash hands after going to the lavatory

✓ 10. Never spit

Source 1

Germs can cause infections. Infections can be viral or bacterial. Examples of viruses are colds, the flu (influenza), chicken pox, or Covid-19. Examples of bacterial infections are strep throat, bacterial meningitis or bacterial pneumonia. Some bacterial infections can be very serious and are often treated with antibiotics. However, antibiotics don't work on viruses.

Antibiotics work by killing bacteria or preventing them from reproducing and spreading. They are effective in easing symptoms and speeding up recovery and they can save lives. However, antibiotics need to be used correctly. Some health professionals are concerned that the over-prescribing of antibiotics is leading to an increasing problem of antibiotic resistance – when antibiotics stop working against bacteria. Nowadays, doctors often make patients wait a while before prescribing antibiotics to see if the infection will clear up on its own.

Activity 1

Design a questionnaire that helps you to find out if the students in your school lead healthy lifestyles. Start by working with another person to come up with five questions that would help you to decide. Don't just think about exercise and 'junk' food. What else affects a person's health?

Activity 2

If we build healthy routines into our lives we can help to keep ourselves and others healthy. Look at the list in Source 1 of what you can do to stop infections spreading. Work with a partner to come up with an example of an infection or disease that might be prevented if you took each action suggested.

Activity 3

How important are teeth to good health?

Activity 4

Is your school a 'healthy school'? Imagine you are giving out awards for this. Work in small groups to think about how you would rate these areas in your school, and give reasons for why you chose these ratings. As judges you are looking at the following areas:

- food
- playgrounds
- getting around the school
- effectiveness of learning opportunities/teaching
- behaviour
- help and support
- taking account of students' views.

Rate each one of these as in the example below.

	Excellent	Good	Not bad	Poor	Awful
Food		✔ *We like the choices – it's good that healthy options are available*			

Activity 5

Look at Source 2. You will be put into groups and each group will take a bit of the 'pie'. Consider your heading from the key and discuss these questions in your groups.

1 What is 'enough sleep'?
2 What is a 'balanced diet'?
3 How much is 'plenty of water'?
4 How much exercise should a person be doing?
5 What should a daily personal hygiene routine include?
6 What are the risks to health of drugs, alcohol and tobacco?

Now, on your own, imagine you're a celebrity with an Instagram account. You share posts to encourage your followers to be healthy. Think about what picture you would share to promote your slice of the pie and what hashtags you would use.
- #5aday
- #8hourssleep
- #freshair

A healthy balance

There are clear dangers in being overweight. There are also links between an inactive lifestyle and ill health, including cancer and cardio-vascular ill-health. And we all need rest and the right amount of sleep too. It is all about balance: a balanced diet and a balanced lifestyle.

- ▨ Have enough sleep
- ▨ Eat a balanced diet
- ☐ Drink plenty of water
- ☐ Take exercise
- ☐ Avoid drugs, alcohol and tobacco
- ▨ Daily personal hygiene routine

Source 2 Healthy and balanced

Teeth

Daily brushing and cleaning between your teeth is important because it removes plaque. If the plaque isn't removed, it continues to build up – feeding on the bits of food left behind and causing tooth decay and gum disease.

Here are five things you can do to keep your teeth healthy:

1 Brush your teeth twice a day
2 Use a fluoride toothpaste
3 Floss your teeth twice a day
4 Limit your intake of high-sugar foods and drinks
5 Visit your dentist twice a year.

Activity 6

What is one new thing you could start doing today to improve your own health?

By the end of 7.2 you will:
- know what 'healthy eating' is
- be able to say what you should eat to keep healthy.

Starter

1 What do you think is meant by 'healthy eating'?
2 Are there foods that we are advised to avoid or cut back on? What should we be including in our diets? What about portion size? And what about drinks?
3 Why is it important to eat healthily? Can young people *choose* to eat healthily?
4 Work with a partner, and list as much as you can think of under the heading 'Healthy eating'.

Activity 1

Why do you think it might be important to plan your meals? Look at Source 1 and make a meal plan for your family for a week.

A Bread, other cereals and potatoes: these should be the basis of most of our meals; they give us energy. These are called **carbohydrates**.

B **Fruit and vegetables**: these contain many of the vitamins and minerals we need for good health; they help us to fight infections, which is very important to healthy eating. Government guidelines say we should be eating five portions of fruit and vegetables each day, but that ten is better!

C Foods containing **saturated fats and sugars**: butter, eggs, cream, oil, biscuits, cakes, ice cream and so on; these should be eaten sparingly. There are also **healthy fats**: nuts, olives, avocados.

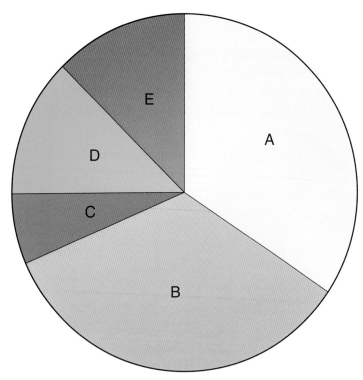

Source 1 This pie chart shows how much of our diet should be taken up by each of the five main food groups.

D **Milk and dairy** foods: milk, cheese, yoghurt; these keep bones and teeth strong and healthy so you should eat moderate amounts.

E Meat, fish, pulses and beans: good sources of **protein**, so eat moderate amounts.

The food traffic light system

If we want to eat healthily, one of the key things we should do is try to cut down on fat (especially saturated fat), salt and added sugars. We need to remember that sugar also causes tooth decay.

With traffic light colours, you can see at a glance if the food you're looking at has high, medium or low amounts of fat, saturated fat, sugars and salt in it (see Source 2).

So, if you see a red light on the front of the pack, you know the food is high in something we should be trying to cut down on. It's fine to have the food occasionally, or as a treat, but try to keep an eye on how often you choose these foods or try eating them in smaller amounts.

Amber means neither high nor low, so you can eat foods with all or mostly amber on the label most of the time.

In short, the more green lights, the healthier the choice.

Red = High

Amber = Medium

Green = Low

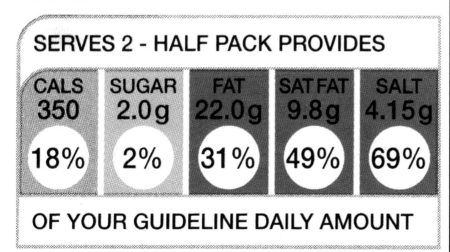

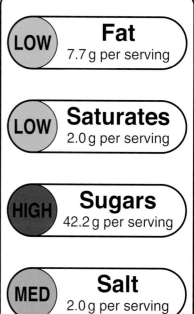

Source 2 Food traffic light system

A balanced diet should include a wide variety of foods from all of the different food groups. It is the combination of these components and nutrients that lead to good health and wellbeing.

Some foods have nutrients added to them that don't naturally occur in the food, these are called 'fortified foods' – they are meant to improve nutrition and add health benefits. For example, bread is often fortified with folic acid, milk with vitamin D and calcium may be added to fruit juices.

Activity 2

Look again at Source 2. Using the system of traffic light colours displayed on foods, suggest how you would plan the family shopping, based on your meal plans from Activity 1.

What are additives?

Sometimes our food has ingredients added to it for taste or to help preserve it for longer, so it is also important to understand these additives and their role in our food and health.

Activity 3

Food Standards Scotland (FSS) has found that some food additives used in hundreds of foods and drinks can cause increased hyperactivity in some children. Read the information in Source 3 and decide which E-numbers you would avoid if shopping for food for children.

If you look on food labels you will often see an 'E' with a number next to it. Most of the processed food we eat would not exist without these additives. You can tell what kind of additive it is by looking at the 'E' number.

E100 to E180	Colouring to make colourless food look more appetising
E200 to E297	Preservatives that artificially make food stay fresh by slowing down the growth of bacteria
E322 to E495	Emulsifiers and stabilisers keep different parts of a food together, for example, air and liquid in ice cream
E620 to E640	Flavourings; some are natural, but artificial ones have E-numbers: they add flavour to food
E950 to E967	Sweeteners used instead of sugar for artificial sweetness

Visit Food Standards Scotland (FSS) at **www.foodstandards.gov. scot** for more information on food additives.

Source 4 E numbers

Source 3 Food additives

Food symbols

Some people have food intolerances or allergies. Some food allergies can be very serious. These people need to read the ingredients on food labels very carefully so that they know exactly what they are eating.

You may see symbols on food or menus like GF, V or VG. What do they mean?

GF means 'gluten-free'. A gluten-free diet is primarily for people with a diagnosed allergy to gluten (coeliac disease) or those who are sensitive or intolerant to it. Excluding the protein gluten (found in wheat, barley or rye) from their diet works as a form of treatment.

V means 'vegetarian' and is used to show that there is no meat or fish. Many people choose not to eat meat or fish. This can be for health or environmental reasons or because they believe in animal rights. Remember that if you aren't eating meat and fish, you need to make sure you're getting protein from other sources, like beans, pulses and lentils or nuts.

VG usually means 'vegan'. Some people choose to eat no meat, fish or animal products. To have good bone health and prevent osteoporosis, you need a diet rich in calcium. Foods rich in calcium include dairy products such as milk, cheese and yoghurts. If you are following a vegan diet, you can drink soya and rice milk fortified with calcium as an alternative to cow's milk. Other non-dairy sources of calcium include tofu, dark green vegetables, kidney beans and dried fruits.

N, a peanut symbol, or a symbol or text saying '**may contain nuts**' can sometimes show that a meal contains nuts. Allergy to nuts is one of the most common allergies in the UK. If someone has a serious nut allergy, they may experience something called anaphylasis, which can cause serious harm and in some cases can be fatal.

Source 5 Checking the label

Source 6 Food packaging should display what allergens the food contains

Obesity

Public health campaigns in the media talk about the problems of obesity. Obesity is a medical condition where fat in the body has increased to such an extent that it may have a negative effect on health.

In Scotland in 2019 around 13 per cent of young people aged 2–16 were obese or at risk of obesity. 28 per cent of those aged 16 or over were considered obese. Unfortunately, the media usually focuses on 'faddy' diets to lose weight rather than healthy eating. Diets based on only one or two foods may be successful in the short term but can be dull and hard to stick to. The healthier, long-term way to lose weight is by eating a healthy, balanced diet and combining it with more physical activity.

Activity 4

Do you think your diet contains too many foods from one group and too little from another? Thinking about what you have learned, how could you achieve more balance in your diet?

By the end of 7.3 you will:
- know the benefits of exercise
- identify the choices you can make to keep healthy.

Starter

All teenagers are different. Many like to spend their free time doing things like shopping, gaming and other online activities whereas others are into reading, watching films and playing sports.

Whatever young people choose to do in their free time, it is often with other people, whether family or friends.

You have a couple of hours free on a Sunday afternoon. You could spend it with family or friends, or both! With a partner, make a list of the things you could do with that time.

Now look at your list and tick the ones that involve being active in some way.

Be prepared to feed back to the class.

Activity 1

We know that exercise is good for us. But are some sports better for us than others? And in what way? Choose one sport and consider its benefits, thinking about:
- aerobic fitness
- muscle tone
- competition
- social benefits.

Prepare a short speech to read out to the class.

The government would like more young people to take up a sport. There are many sports clubs that young people can join. But how do you find out about them? A good start would be to speak to someone at school in the PE department, or check the PE department notice board.

Activity 2

How do you get to school? Conduct a survey like the one in Source 1 to find out if anyone in your class walks or cycles to school. For those that don't walk or cycle, ask them why not.

Activity 3

Walking or cycling to school is a good way to get daily fresh air and exercise. It also reduces traffic congestion in towns and the area around a school so has a positive environmental impact too. Take a look at the reasons why students in your class choose not to walk or cycle to school. Can any of these reasons be helped? Is there anything that can be done by your school or your local community to solve these issues and allow more students to walk or cycle?

Participant	Walk or Cycle	Reason for 'No'
1	Yes – cycle	
2	No	Too far
3	No	No pavement to walk on
4	Yes – walk	
5	Yes – walk	
6	No	Parents won't allow me to walk or cycle
7	No	Don't have a bike
8	Yes – cycle	
9	No	Nowhere to change/shower if cycle
10	No	Too much to carry

Source 1 Survey

Activity 4

Some people like the challenge that a sport offers: the goal setting to achieve personal bests; or they enjoy the competition. You don't need to join a sports club for a challenge; you can set yourself challenges. For example, you could use a pedometer or a phone app and see if you can increase your daily steps, or see how long you can keep a football up for when playing 'keepy-uppy' in the back garden.

Can you think of an active challenge?

Many charities hold sponsored walks, runs, swims or cycles that you could get involved in. This would mean you get some exercise, set yourself a challenge and raise some money for charity at the same time! Some schools or organisations, like the Scouts or local youth clubs, allow young people to start their Duke of Edinburgh's Award (DofE) in Third Year (S3). There are also DofE open Award centres in most towns. If you get the chance to do your DofE, there is a physical section and an expedition which can involve walking, cycling, kayaking, horse riding, and so on.

How much should I be doing?

For children and young people, physical activity includes play, games, sports, transportation, chores, recreation, physical education, or planned exercise, in the context of family, school, and community activities.

1 Children and youths aged 5–17 should accumulate at least 60 minutes of moderate- to vigorous-intensity physical activity daily.
2 Amounts of physical activity greater than 60 minutes provide additional health benefits.
3 Most of the daily physical activity should be aerobic.

Source 2 The World Health Organization (WHO) makes recommendations for children and young people aged 5–17

Activity 5

Read Source 2. With a partner, work out how much daily physical activity you each have. Remember to include breaktimes at school, PE learning opportunities, walking to and from school and planned sporting activities on a school day. Do you do more or less at weekends and why? Do you think you are taking enough exercise?

Activity 6

In pairs, list the benefits of exercise. Include the benefits to physical health but also mental health, and any social and environmental benefits that might be found from walking to school with friends, for example. Then put them in an order of importance. Be prepared to feed back to the class.

Activity 7

Reflect on today's learning opportunity. Are there any changes that you plan to make to your weekly routine in order to take more exercise?

By the end of 7.4 you will:
- know what's in place to support both world health and personal health (including screening, immunisation, and so on)
- identify the choices you can make to keep healthy.

Starter

Your life involves making choices. Think back over the day so far, from the time you woke up until now. What choices have you made today that could affect your health? These could be choices about washing, food, exercise and so on.

It is important that the maintenance of a healthy lifestyle is built in to daily routine. It requires thought and planning. For instance, getting up in the morning in time to have breakfast, wash or shower and clean your teeth, making sure you have something for lunch and a water bottle, plus allowing time to walk to school, if possible, is a good start to the day!

Teenagers are spending an increasing amount of time in extracurricular activities such as dance classes, drama clubs and sports. They're also working hard at homework and often other extra studies. All this is important, but so is getting enough rest to do it all.

A daily routine is important. So is a healthy diet and a good balance between work, play, exercise and rest!

The importance of sleep

Most teenagers need eight to nine hours of sleep each night. Getting the right amount of sleep is essential for anyone who wants to concentrate in class, sit a test or do well in a sport. Unfortunately, though, many teenagers don't get enough sleep.

Experts say that during the teenage years, the body's sleep rhythms are temporarily reset, telling teenagers to fall asleep later and wake up later. This change might be because the brain hormone melatonin is produced later at night for teenagers than it is for children and adults. Are you getting enough sleep?

Activity 1

1. What are the signs and symptoms of someone not getting enough sleep?
2. What suggestions could you make to help someone plan to get more sleep?

How does immunisation work?

Vaccines work by stimulating the body's immune system to make antibodies (substances to fight infections and diseases). So if you come into contact with the infection, the antibodies will recognise it and protect you – and you will therefore be **immunised**.

By the time you have become a teenager, the NHS will have asked you and your family to think about a range of immunisations. The national immunisation programme has meant that dangerous diseases such as tetanus, diphtheria and polio have practically disappeared in the UK. But these diseases could come back – they still exist in Europe and throughout the world. That's why it's so important for you to protect yourself.

Activity 2

Look at Source 1. Some of you will have had or are soon going to have the HPV vaccine (see 12–13 years in the table). Use a website like **www.nhsinform.scot/healthy-living/immunisation** or another source to find the answers to the following questions:
1 What is HPV?
2 Who is entitled to the HPV vaccine in the UK?
3 What does the vaccine do?

Age	Vaccine
2 months	5-in-1 vaccine – this single jab protects against: diphtheria, tetanus, pertussis (whooping cough), polio and Hib type B (a bacterial infection that can cause severe pneumonia or meningitis in young children) Pneumonia vaccine Rotavirus vaccine
3 months	5-in-1 vaccine, second dose Meningitis C Rotavirus vaccine, second dose
4 months	5-in-1 vaccine, third dose Pneumonia vaccine, second dose
Between 12 and 13 months	Hib/Meningitis C booster, given as a single jab Measles, mumps and rubella (MMR) vaccine Pneumonia vaccine, third dose
2 to 3 years	Flu vaccine (annual)
3 years and 4 months, or soon after	Measles, mumps and rubella (MMR) vaccine, second dose 4-in-1 pre-school booster: single jab containing vaccines against diphtheria, tetanus, whooping cough (pertussis) and polio
Around 12 to 13 years	HPV vaccine
Around 13 to 15 years	Meningitis C booster
Around 13 to 18 years	3-in-1 teenage booster: single jab vaccines against diphtheria, tetanus and polio
Age 65 and over	Flu (every year) Pneumonia vaccine

Source 1 Typical UK immunisation programme

World health and immunisation

SUSTAINABLE DEVELOPMENT G⚙ALS

Source 2 The Sustainable Development Goals (SDGs)

> The Sustainable Development Goals are a collection of 17 global goals set by the United Nations General Assembly in 2015 to be achieved by 2030.

Access to immunisation is essential if we are to achieve the Sustainable Development Goals (SDGs) by 2030. Getting rid of disease helps priorities like SDG#4 Quality Education and SDG#8 Economic Growth to take hold.

It could be argued that immunisation is the most cost-effective preventive health intervention. The international community has frequently stressed the value of vaccines and immunisation to prevent and control a large number of infectious diseases and, increasingly, several chronic diseases that are caused by infectious agents.

On average each year, about 85 per cent of infants worldwide receive a vaccine which protects them against infectious diseases that can cause serious illness and disability or be fatal. Yet an additional 1.5 million deaths could be avoided if global immunisation coverage was improved.

A teenager has told how he secretly got vaccinated against the wishes of his parents, who he claimed believed debunked anti-vaccine "conspiracy theories", they read on the internet.

Ethan Lindenberger, 18, appealed for help on a Reddit forum, asking which vaccines he should obtain,

as he said he had never received any, because "my parents are kind of stupid and don't believe in vaccines". "God knows how I'm still alive," he wrote.

After reading the advice, the teenager obtained vaccines for hepatitis A, hepatitis B, influenza and HPV.

Source 3 This article describes a fairly rare case, in which an 18 year old researched vaccinations himself. What else might he have done? What other advice could he have sought?

Activity 3

1 What type of health tests have you been offered? Possibly eye tests and hearing tests? How important is it to go for these?
2 Some people are offered screening for certain health problems. Screening is a way of finding out if people are at higher risk of a health problem, so that early treatment can be offered or information given to help them make informed decisions. What are the pros and cons of screening?

Antibiotics

Antibiotics are medicines that are used to prevent and treat bacterial infections. Antibiotic resistance happens when bacteria change in response to the use of antibiotics. It's the bacteria, not humans or animals, that become antibiotic-resistant. These bacteria may infect humans and animals, and the infections they cause are harder to treat than those caused by non-resistant bacteria. We need to change the way we use antibiotics. We also need to reduce the spread of infections through vaccination, hand washing, practising safe sex, and good food hygiene.

Activity 4

What is the one thing you would remove from the world that would instantly make it a healthier place? Why?

7.5 When health goes wrong

By the end of 7.5 you will:
- understand your rights to health and treatment
- know some facts about blood, organ and stem cell donation.

Starter

What do the letters **NHS** stand for?

As under 16s you get services, like an eye test at an opticians or a dental check-up at the dentist, for free. If you visit your GP (your family doctor) and you need medicine, your doctor will give you a prescription to take to a chemist to pick up the medicine. Prescriptions are free in Scotland.

An A&E (Accident and Emergency) department (also known as emergency department or casualty) deals with genuine life-threatening emergencies, such as:

- loss of consciousness
- acute confused state and fits that are not stopping
- chest pain
- breathing difficulties
- severe bleeding that cannot be stopped
- severe allergic reactions
- severe burns or scalds
- stroke
- major trauma such as a road traffic accident.

Less severe injuries can be treated in urgent care centres or minor injuries clinics. A&E is not an alternative to a GP appointment. If your GP surgery is closed you can phone NHS 24 Scotland on 111 and they will direct you to the best local service or give you advice. Alternatively, you can visit an NHS urgent treatment or walk-in centre, which will also treat minor illnesses without an appointment.

It is important to learn how to administer basic first aid. This is now taught in most schools or with St Andrew's First Aid. It is also important to carry out self-examination (of breasts and testicles, in particular) and attend screening as required.

One of the situations where we want confidential care is when we see someone about personal health problems. Young people under 16 are entitled to have their confidential information treated in exactly the same way as adults. Your health care will more often than not be something you happily discuss with your parents or carers. However, sometimes you may wish to discuss things in private.

Activity 1

Where would you go or what would you do in these situations?
a Your five-year-old brother has fallen off a climbing frame and bumped his head.
b You have a very heavy cold and you just feel generally unwell.
c Your friend has cut their elbow and it is bleeding.
d Your aunt is having severe chest pains.
e You have eczema behind your knees and it is getting worse.

Activity 2

Your teacher has mentioned the word 'confidentiality' in PSE learning opportunities. In pairs, come up with a definition of the word 'confidentiality'. Be prepared to share it with the class so that you can agree upon a class definition.

a) At what age can I see a doctor on my own?

b) Can I choose my own doctor?

c) Can I be sure that I'll be treated in confidence by a nurse or doctor?

d) Can I get confidential advice about anything to do with sex if I am under sixteen?

Source 1

Activity 3

Look at Source 1. The questions in the speech bubbles are often asked by young people who are unsure of their rights. In groups, consider these worries. What would you say to reassure each questioner? You could use the NHS (Scotland) fact sheet found at **www.nhsinform.scot/publications/confidentiality-your-rights-factsheet** to help you answer some of these questions.

Activity 4

Write a letter to the editor of your local newspaper in which you persuade the readers to become blood donors or join a bone marrow registry. Use Source 2 to help you.

About defibrillators

You might see a defibrillator like the one in Source 4 in a public space like an airport or a shopping centre. You might even have one in your school. These defibrillators are called public access defibrillators or PADs for short. A defibrillator is a device that gives a high energy electric shock to the heart of someone whose heart has stopped beating. When someone's heart has stopped beating, we say that they are in cardiac arrest. A cardiac arrest can happen to anyone, at any time. This high energy electric shock is called defibrillation and might save someone's life.

If you come across someone who is in cardiac arrest, you should follow the steps in Source 3.

Blood and organ donation

- There is a constant demand for donated blood, but only about 4 per cent of the people in the UK who can give blood do so.
- The number of people needing an organ transplant was far greater than the number of organs being donated. So during 2020 the law changed so that all people over 16 will be presumed to be organ donors unless they opt out.
- In the UK, people are still dying while waiting for a bone marrow transplant.

Source 2 Fact file

1 Call 999. Give as much information as possible. The call handler may be able to direct you to the nearest defibrillator.
2 Check: the person's airways for obstruction; their breathing; and their circulation.
3 If the person is not breathing and does not respond, start CPR (see 8.8 First Aid and CPR).
4 Ask someone to fetch a defibrillator, if there's one nearby.
5 Turn the defibrillator on and follow its instructions.

The video at the link below also gives helpful advice on how to use a defibrillator.
www.youtube.com/watch?v=Tqf6QI3ZWwk

Source 3

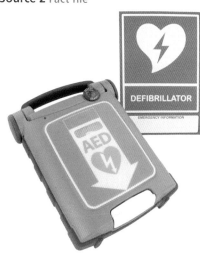

Source 4 A defibrillator

By the end of 8.1 you will:
- **understand what 'risk' can mean**
- **understand what is meant by 'risking on purpose'**
- **be aware of online risks.**

Starter

Look at Source 1. In pairs, discuss whether Homer is right.

'Trying is the first step towards failure.' - Homer Simpson

Source 1 Do you believe Homer is right?

Everything you do in life has the possibility of a good or bad outcome – you can think of these as positive or negative risks.

A positive risk is one where you are doing something because you hope that you will gain something, improve yourself or enjoy yourself. An example might be speaking in front of the class – this may improve your communication skills and build your confidence.

A negative risk is one with an outcome that could harm you or someone else. An example might be drinking alcohol before riding a bike or driving a car – this can put you and others in danger.

When we think about reducing risks, we are probably thinking about the harm that taking that risk might cause. So we need to think about two things:

- the *what* – the harm that might happen to us
- the *might* – the likelihood that harm will happen to us.

Take the example of an aeroplane crash. The chance of being harmed if an aeroplane crashes is high. However, the likelihood of this happening is low, because so few planes crash compared with the large numbers that fly every day. So, would you fly in a plane?

Crossing a busy road

Smoking cigarettes

Source 2 Risky, or not?

Activity 1

Look at Source 2. Do these photos suggest anything about 'risk' to you? If so, what? Share your ideas with someone else.

Activity 2

Can you think of any other examples that show the difference between the 'what' and the 'might'? Here's an idea to get you started:

Activity	What ...	Might ...
Bungee jumping	Bungee snaps	Highly unlikely if equipment is regularly checked, assessed and the company is professionally validated

THE EXPERIENCE CENTRE

We can offer you the time of your life and get your adrenalin buzzing! Try the most scary thrills – feel the fear and do it anyway!

White-water rafting   Zip-wire   Go-karting

Source 3 Taking risks

Wanting to take risks on purpose is natural and is how we learn to progress in life. It helps us to understand our own boundaries and build our resilience.

At an activity centre people will want to try different things, some appearing more risky than others. Health and safety rules are important at an activity centre, as risks need to be assessed and managed.

Some people enjoy taking personal risks by doing extreme sports or going on wild adventure holidays. We also need to assess risks in our day-to-day lives: when we go to cross a road, we need to stop, look left and right, and listen, and then assess the risk before crossing. But how about online risks? The internet is amazing: it gives everyone who has internet access an endless supply of knowledge, information and entertainment, but using it comes with risks.

Activity 3

What does the expression 'taking a positive risk' mean?

Imagine your year group is planning a day at the Experience Centre in Source 3. Your teachers will have completed a thorough risk assessment – and they also want you to think about how to plan an event like this. Discuss the topic you have been given, weigh up the risks and then present your findings as a brilliant challenge rather than a potential nightmare.

Activity 4

Work with a partner and create a list of the risks that we take whenever we go online. Be prepared to share these with the class.

More information about safety online can be found at www.saferinternet.org.uk.

Activity 5

Before today's learning opportunity you may only have thought of risk as a negative thing. What is the best positive risk you have taken?

By the end of 8.2 you will:
- be able to identify some ways to keep yourself safe on- and offline.

Starter

Think back to the previous learning opportunity and remind yourself of the meaning of the word 'risk'. What definition would you give?

Activity 1

Where do you think you are most at risk?

Here are four locations where accidents might happen to someone your age:
- on the road or in car parks
- in or around the home
- in school
- on a sports field/in a sports hall (while doing sport).

Where do you think an accident is most likely to happen? Rank the locations in order of most dangerous to least dangerous.

Activity 2

Look at the situations in Source 1. What would you do?

It isn't always obvious when we might be at risk – we need to think and plan to keep safe. This will help us reduce the risk of something bad happening. Risk can never be completely ruled out – but there are ways in which we can think about a situation and reduce the risks.

It's a sunny day in the summer holidays and you and your friends are spending the day in the park. Some of the group decide that climbing to the top of one of the trees would be a great idea.

You have spent the day at a friend's house. You have been told you have to be back home by 6 p.m. You thought you had allowed plenty of time but you've missed the bus and the battery has died on your mobile phone. It's getting late. You know you're going to be in trouble if you're not home on time.

You and your friends are at a party. Everyone is helping themselves to food and drink. People are behaving as if they are a bit drunk. You want to keep in with everyone in your group but you don't want to drink alcohol. One of your mates offers you a bottle of something alcoholic.

Source 1 Risky situations?

Activity 3

In Activity 2 you looked at how you could deal with risky situations that could arise. However, there are some sensible precautions we could all take to keep ourselves safe.

Look at the safety suggestions in Source 2. Put each of them under one of the following three headings:
- Travelling safely
- Feeling under threat
- Looking after personal possessions

Be careful if you're using the latest phone model, iPod, etc. in public places – expensive equipment could attract potential thieves and muggers.

If you are threatened, yell and run away, if possible.

Never hitchhike or take rides from strangers and try to avoid walking home alone.

Avoid taking short-cuts through dark or deserted places.

Don't walk around outside listening on headphones as this prevents you being aware of what is happening around you.

If someone approaches you asking directions and they make you feel uncomfortable, keep your distance or walk away.

If you are being followed, go into a shop or towards people or try crossing the road to see if the person follows.

Source 2 Safety suggestions. Information from the charity Kidscape and teenagers in conversation

Activity 4

You are at, or approaching, the age when you may choose to sign up to a social networking site. We can reduce some of the risks online by making sure we have good privacy settings when we use social media. Working in pairs, create a table, with one column for what you would post on a private profile, and the other on a public profile. For example, where would you post these?
- photo of favourite band
- email address
- picture of your sister's new baby.

Activity 5

Here are some recommendations that are worth considering, in order to reduce risks online. Discuss these with a partner. Why is it important to follow these guidelines?
- Be as anonymous as possible.
- Protect your personal information.
- Be honest about your age.
- Think before posting any photos that identify you and where you live/go to school, and so on.
- Avoid meeting someone that you have only met online.
- Check 'friend requests' carefully before accepting.
- Check your profile or page regularly for comments.

Can you think of any more? Be prepared to feed back to the class.

Activity 6

Now, on your own, write an acrostic using the phrase B.E. S.A.F.E. O.N.L.I.N.E.

Each letter needs to begin a sentence giving important advice on internet safety.

Activity 7

Think about how you would complete this sentence:

The most important safety message I've learned from today's learning opportunity is … because …

Share your sentence with one other person.

By the end of 8.3 you will:
- **know how to use good communication skills to help reduce risks**
- **be able to demonstrate strategies to deal with pressure from others.**

Starter

Look at Source 1. Can you think of a time when you have not wanted to go along with what friends have wanted, but have done so just to please them? For example, your friends asked you to go out one evening but all you wanted to do was to stay at home with your family. Why did you still go out with your friends?

Standing up to, disagreeing with or saying 'no' to your friends is not easy. This might be because we don't want to hurt their feelings, or we might feel left out or different from the group. It is about being 'assertive' but not 'aggressive'.

It is natural to want to go along with what somebody else wants to please them. On the other hand, if they care about you, they will understand you have your own feelings and wishes. Remember: looking after yourself and paying attention to your own feelings is not necessarily selfish.

Source 1 Why is it so hard to say 'no'?

Activity 1

1 What things have you said 'no' to?
2 What have other people said 'no' to you about?
3 Is it important to be able to say 'no'?

In Activity 1 you discussed how it can be difficult to say 'no' in a variety of situations and to various people. There are some clear ways of communicating with people that mean we don't have to end up doing something we don't want to do. These are:

- actively listening to the other person

- being assertive

- using refusal skills – we use these when we feel we might be harmed or in danger.

Read Source 2 for some simple techniques for saying 'no'.

How to say 'no'

- Simply say 'no' or 'no thanks'.
- Be direct, for example, 'No, I don't want to do that.'
- Be a broken record – repeat 'no' over and over again or use variations to make your point: 'No, I'm not interested', 'Not me!', 'No, never'.
- Walk away – if they won't accept your 'no' then it's time to go!
- 'I know that you really want to do that, but it's not something that interests me.'
- 'Thanks for asking but I don't want to do that today.'
- 'I can see that this is something you feel strongly about, but I don't want to do that.'

Source 2

Activity 2

Imagine that one of your really good friends asks you to join in with something you don't want to do, saying 'I think you'll really enjoy this. Give it a try.'

Come up with five different sentences that you could use to refuse them. Make sure your responses are calm, assertive and polite.

Activity 3

Refusal skills are part of a range of ways that we can communicate to keep ourselves safe and to reduce risks. Give yourself a rating for how well you think you can use these three different communication skills:

	I can do this really well	I'm fairly good at this	I need to practise this more
Active listening			
Being assertive			
Saying 'no'			

It is important to follow your own instinct. If you think that something is the right thing to do, then it probably is! Likewise, if you feel uncomfortable with a decision that you have made, then it probably was the wrong thing to do.

Go with your gut instinct and don't bow to peer pressure. Remember that you have to live with any decisions you have made. This also applies to being a bystander. If you see someone struggling, and it is clear they need or want help, and you can ensure your own safety – then be an 'active bystander' and help them.

Activity 4

Your teacher will give you some scenarios where someone (A) is trying to persuade someone else (B) to do something that is not the most sensible course of action. Take it in turns to play the roles, A (the persuader) and B (the asserter). B will need to be assertive in their tone and might also need to be persuasive, perhaps suggesting other courses of action and not just saying 'no'.

After you have role played the conversation both ways, give your partner feedback on the good things they did to demonstrate that they could be assertive without being aggressive.

Activity 5

Look back over the scenarios described in Activity 4 where someone might need to stand up for what they think is right. Can you suggest any more scenarios?

By the end of 8.4 you will:

- be able to identify strategies for the prevention of bullying, including cyberbullying
- understand the importance of speaking out against bullying.

Everyone – young people, teachers, adults – can help put a stop to bullying.

There are lots of reasons why some people start bullying and why they choose certain people to target. Those who choose to bully others will focus on something about another person in order to belittle and hurt them; this could be their appearance, personality, behaviour … However, bullying, at school or outside school, off- or online, is always wrong, no matter what.

Freddie's story

We had this PE teacher and he thought anyone who wasn't good at games was stupid. I'm really small for my age and not much good at PE. He started picking on me in learning opportunities. Then he started calling me a wimp and other things. It doesn't sound much. I mean, he never touched me or pushed me around or anything, so when I tried to tell my mum, it did sound rather pathetic.

Source 1

Jojo's story

It all started when my mum got married again. I liked my new step-sister. She was the same age as me and I thought we could be friends. When she moved in, though, her friends came round all the time and made life difficult for me. She kept putting me down with comments about how I looked. She said if I told Mum I'd be in trouble and I'd split the family up. Then she started threatening me and saying that if I didn't do her homework for her she'd tell Mum I was calling her names. I did try talking to Mum but she was so happy I didn't want to spoil things for her.

Source 2

Tam's story

I was new at the school – joining halfway through the year – and break times were the worst. This group of students used to hang around by these seats that were out of sight of the school windows, and that's why they went there. At first, they were friendly and chatty and, being new, I was really pleased that they let me be part of their group. Then they wanted me to buy stuff for them. I said I didn't want to and that's when it started. They got all the other students in the class to completely blank me and then they started sending horrible messages to me. Then someone hacked into my online profile and made stuff up about me.

Source 3

Starter

There is never a justifiable reason for bullying. Ever.

Bullying at school can happen for lots of reasons. Why do bullies single people out? What sort of things do they pick on?

Activity 1

Read Sources 1, 2 and 3 about young people's experiences of being bullied. Suggest three ways in which each young person could begin to tackle their situation: consider how these young people might be feeling and what impact bullying is having on them in both the short and the long term.

Activity 2

1. How do you think your school creates a positive atmosphere in which students support and help each other? Are there additional things that you can suggest?
2. In and around school, what could students do to prevent bullying happening in the first place? How can a school create an ethos of respect?

> I knew the photo was faked. It was horrible and stupid, but if I didn't take part in sending it round I knew they'd do the same to me.

> He showed me the text message he'd got. It was really mean.

> My friend went on and on about being bullied – I got tired of listening to her.

> There weren't any adults around when it was happening.

Source 4 Bystanders' words

Apathetic bystanders are people who do not act while someone else is being bullied. They are not the ringleaders but sometimes they may join in with name calling. Bullying behaviour can be fuelled by the action, or lack of action, of the bystander.

Cyberbullying

Cyberbullying is any form of bullying which takes place online.

Think about some of the social networking sites, messaging apps, gaming sites and chatrooms that you know or maybe even use. Although using them might be fun and a positive experience, there is a downside: anything nasty posted about you can spread and be seen by lots of people. Sometimes, unpleasant things can be spread by people who were once your best friends so it's better to keep secrets and personal information to yourself. Only tell people things if it wouldn't embarrass you if other people found out about them.

Remember: posting false and malicious things about people on the internet can be classed as harassment. If you post abuse about anyone else online or if you send threats, you can be traced by the police easily. Every time you visit a website or make a posting, your internet service provider has an electronic note of your activity. Even if you create an anonymous email address, you can still be traced.

Being bullied online can impact on a person's self-esteem, confidence and social skills. Always consider the impact your words may have and think twice before posting.

In fact, think twice before you post anything online because once it's out there you can't take it back. It is easy for any comments or posts you make online to be taken out of context and these could be damaging to you in the future.

Activity 3

Have you ever seen bullying happening and not known what to do? Look at Source 4 – these are statements from young people who were bystanders. What would you say to each bystander to encourage them to help?

Activity 4

More information about safety online can be found at **www.saferinternet.org.uk**.

Go to the 'Advice and resources' section and choose your age group. How do the suggestions in this section help somebody deal with bullying online?

Activity 5

Think of a slogan to highlight the responsibilities of bystanders to report bullying.

By the end of 8.5 you will:
- understand what 'gambling' means
- be able to explain the risks attached to gambling.

Starter

What does 'gambling' mean? Draw a mind map and write down any words that you think of when you hear the word 'gambling'.

- National Lottery – you can buy, play and sell National Lottery tickets and scratch cards from the age of sixteen.
- Football pools – you can bet on the pools from the age of sixteen.
- Bingo – you are allowed into a bingo club at any age but have to be eighteen or over to participate.
- Betting shop – no one under eighteen is allowed on the premises or to place a bet.
- Casinos – you are not allowed into a casino under the age of eighteen.
- Gaming machines – children under eighteen can only play low-stake, low pay-out machines – often found in seaside arcades or theme parks.
- Online/mobile gambling via the internet or an app – also comes under the legislation restricting this to adults: you are not allowed to play if you are under eighteen.

Source 1 Gambling, the law and you: The Gambling Act 2005. There have been amendments since 2005 but no changes to minimum ages for gambling.

Activity 1

Read Source 1, then read Source 2 which gives facts on young people's attitudes towards gambling and gamblers, and what their influences are when choosing to gamble or not.

In pairs, discuss these questions:
1 Why do some people choose to gamble?
2 Why do some people choose not to gamble?

Attitudes and influences (based on young people aged 11–16 living in Britain):
- 59% agree that gambling is dangerous and only 14% agree that it is OK for someone their age to gamble
- Almost half of young people (49%) said that someone had spoken to them about the problems gambling may lead to
- 66% of young people have seen gambling adverts on TV, 59% on social media and 53% on other websites
- 49% had seen or heard TV or radio programmes sponsored by a gambling company and 46% had encountered gambling sponsorships at sports venues
- 7% claimed that they had been prompted to gamble by a gambling advert or sponsorship
- More than one in ten young people (12%) follow gambling companies on social media

Source 2 From 'Young people and gambling 2018' by The Gambling Commission

One way to define gambling is: it usually involves two or more people risking a stake (usually money or other valuables) on an uncertain outcome, which is partly determined by chance. The stake is paid by the loser to the winner.

Paul Bellringer, Director of Responsible Gambling Solutions

Activity 2

Look at Source 3.
1 What is happening in the cartoon?
2 What amazing things do pop-up adverts offer people on the internet?
3 Why do gambling websites use pop-ups?

Source 3 **Pop-up gambling?**

1. Steph has moved to a seaside town, just in time for the start of the new school year. There is an amusement arcade on the pier which has a number of the 'coin-pusher' and 'claw' machines. One afternoon, Steph visited the pier and caught sight of the arcade. Steph had some 2p coins and so decided to have a go on one of the 'coin-pusher' machines. Winning streak! Steph changed some other coins and kept playing. Steph had enjoyed playing on the machines, so went back each day until the term started. There were 10p machines too and a 'claw' machine where you can win soft toys or money. Once the new term had begun, Steph could pop into the arcade on the way home from school. It was difficult to stop playing each day as Steph always felt lucky! Unfortunately, school dinner money and pocket money does not stretch very far...

2. Lucas and his friends enjoyed playing football outside, pretty much whatever the weather! Occasionally though, they would go to someone's house and play online games or cards, or watch sport on the telly. Today they were meeting at Liam's house to hang out and watch the football later. Liam's older brother was placing a bet online on the outcome of the match. Liam said that he usually got his brother to put money on for him too and suggested that they all put in £1 to place a larger bet. Lucas had never gambled before but gave Liam £1. They didn't win anything! However, some of the friends enjoyed the excitement and tension of betting and suggested that they do this weekly and each put in £5...

3. Ava was saving up for a music festival ticket. 'Early bird' tickets for locals were being released on Friday. If she didn't have enough money then, it was unlikely she would be able to afford a ticket when they come out on general sale. At lunch in the canteen, she overheard some other students saying how someone had won some money on a scratchcard and that they were nearly able to buy a festival ticket outright with their winnings! Ava was desperate to go to the festival. On her way home she popped in to the shop and saw the scratchcards at the counter...

Source 4

Activity 3

In pairs, read the scenarios in Source 4 and make a note of what issues there are to consider. Be prepared to feed back to the class.

Activity 4

People have very different attitudes to gambling.

In Source 2 you read: '59% (of 11–16 year olds living in Britain) agree that gambling is dangerous and only 14% agree that it is OK for someone their age to gamble.'
1 Do you think gambling is dangerous?
2 Is it OK for someone of your age to gamble?

Activity 5

How have your attitudes towards gambling changed as a result of this learning opportunity?

By the end of 8.6 you will:
- **know how to carry out research and present your findings on issues which may affect people of your age**
- **understand the impact of knife crime and gangs on society: locally, nationally and globally.**

The learning opportunity is designed to be a starting point for you, to open up an initial discussion about the topic of gangs and knife crime, and what effects it can have on you and the wider community. It covers issues which may affect the personal safety of people your age. You may already know about these issues or you may not have thought about them. They can affect people in all kinds of communities and situations – not just in large cities, or in groups that the media choose to highlight.

Your teacher may then decide to use this learning opportunity as a basis for future ones, where you might look in more detail at this complex issue.

Knife crime

> Just to know that your son or daughter went out to have a good time … and then they don't come home. You don't think that's ever going to happen.

> I had high hopes for him. I never thought he would carry a knife.

> Saying you carried it for defence can't be an excuse.

> Friends and family are always left to pick up the pieces.

Source 1 Knife crime

FAQ

Q. I am 14. Can I buy a knife?

A. In Scotland, you cannot buy any type of knife if you're under 16 years old. If you are 16 or older you may purchase knives for domestic use. If you are under 18, it is against the law to sell any knife, knife blade, open razor blade, axe, sword or any other article that has a blade or is sharply pointed and is made or adapted so that it could cause injury or harm to people. There are some types of knife which are illegal for anyone to buy, like flick knives. If you are carrying a knife in a public place, you can be arrested by police. If police officers have reasonable grounds to suspect that you are carrying a knife, they can stop and search you. In England, Wales and Northern Ireland, the laws are similar but if you're under the age of 18 you're not allowed to buy any knife, including kitchen knives.

Source 2 Knife crime and the law

Starter

Look at Source 1.
Apart from the victim and the offender, think about who else is affected by the issue:
a locally
b nationally
c globally.

Activity 1

Knife crime in the UK is on the increase. Read the FAQ and newspaper headlines in Sources 2 and 3. Discuss whether you would change any laws or police powers relating to buying and carrying knives.

One boy killed and another injured in east London stabbings

Co-op curbs sale of knives in response to rising crime

Scottish approach to knife crime applauded for considering the problem a health and education issue

Source 3 Newspaper headlines

Gangs

What is a gang?

Police define a gang as:

A group of people who spend time in public places that:

- see themselves (and are seen by others) as a noticeable group, and
- engage in a range of criminal activity and violence.

They may also have any or all of the following features:

- identify with or lay a claim over territory
- are in conflict with other, similar gangs.

However, if the majority of offending is of a lower, non-violent level then they would be considered a peer group not a gang.

Activity 2

Discuss how you feel after reading Sources 4, 5 and 6.

I don't know who to turn to for help. 'I really want to leave a life in gangs behind. But I feel that there is nobody out there who cares about young people like me. I don't think I can do this on my own.'

Source 5 Jay

Like celebrities, influencers and politicians, gang members face pressure to continue being 'the best' by being the most talked about – and outdoing themselves each time. Violence has long had a 'display value' and has always been deployed as a means of achieving status on the streets, but on the 'digital street' conflict is king. Physical conflicts used to be temporally and geographically limited. Now, perceived taunts and insults remain live and can be replayed indefinitely, as well as being seen by a large audience of friends and followers. This pressure to perform creates incentives to respond and retaliate, ultimately leading to an escalating prospect of real violence taking place.

Source 6 Gangs and social media.
Adapted from *The Guardian*,
15 January 2019

Headline News

You can be ex-gang but you can never be an ex-murderer

Nicola Dyer shakes with bitter anger as she describes the fatal stabbing of her 16-year-old son Shakilus Townsend in a trap staged by London gang members four years ago.

The youngsters, identified by police as being linked to street crime, stop slouching in front of Nicola. They are attentive. The mum of five tells them:

'Five years ago my son was killed. He was chased down in the street like he was an animal, and then stabbed and beaten to death.

'Young people talk about joining a gang as being like a family, but I would like to know what sort of family you get from that? What kind of family would beat and stab somebody?

'You have one chance to make something of your lives.

'You can be ex-gang members, but you can't be ex-murderers.'

Source 4 Adapted from *The Mirror*, 23 July 2013

By the end of 8.7 you will:
- have some understanding of the concepts of, and laws relating to, female genital mutilation, or FGM.

Starter

Read Source 1, which is an extract from a memoir called *Desert Flower* by Waris Dirie. What was Aman going to have done?

Waris refers to the procedure she is going to have as 'female circumcision'. However, the more commonly term used in the UK is female genital mutilation. Why do you think this is the preferred term for this procedure?

Why do you think Waris was so keen to have this procedure done?

Becoming a woman (part 1)

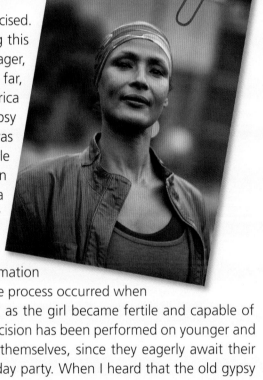

The time had come for my oldest sister, Aman, to be circumcised. Like all younger siblings, I was jealous that she was entering this grownup world that was still closed to me. Aman was a teenager, much older than the normal age for circumcision, but so far, the timing had never been right. As my family travelled Africa in an endless cycle, we had somehow missed the gypsy woman who performed this ancient ritual. My father was growing concerned, because Aman was reaching marriageable age, but no marriage could take place unless she had been properly 'fixed'. The actual details of the ritual are left a mystery – it's never explained to the girls. You just know that something special is going to happen to you when your time comes. As a result, all young girls in my country anxiously await the ceremony that will make their transformation from being a little girl to becoming a woman. Originally the process occurred when the girls reach puberty, and the ritual had some meaning, as the girl became fertile and capable of bearing her own children. But through time, female circumcision has been performed on younger and younger girls, partially due to the pressure from the girls themselves, since they eagerly await their 'special time' as a child in the West might await her birthday party. When I heard that the old gypsy was coming to circumcise Aman, I wanted to be circumcised too. The day before the event, I begged my mother, tugging at her arm, 'Mama, do us both together. Come on Mama, do both of us tomorrow'.

Source 1 Extract from *Desert Flower* by Waris Dirie

What is FGM?

Female genital mutilation (FGM) refers to 'all procedures involving partial or total removal of the external female genitalia or other injury to the female genital organs for non-medical reasons.' (World Health Organization 2008) There are four types of FGM:

- Type 1 (clitoridectomy) – This is the partial or total removal of the clitoris.
- Type 2 (excision) – This is the partial or total removal of the clitoris and the inner lips (labia minora).
- Type 3 (infibulation) – This is the partial or total removal of the clitoris and inner and outer lips (labia minora and labia majora), and the sewing together of the outer lips or the remaining skin to leave a smooth layer of scar tissue covering the genitals. A small hole is left to allow urine and menstrual blood to flow out of the body.
- Type 4 – This covers a wide range of practices found across the world, and includes pricking, burning, stretching of the labia, scraping and piercing of the female genitals.

Why is it called FGM?

It is called FGM because of the harm it causes to girls' and women's bodies, health and wellbeing, and because there is no medical reason for doing it. FGM is also sometimes called female circumcision and it may also be known by other names used by different communities: Bondo, Kutairi, Halalays, Gudiniin and many others. Remember, no matter what it is called, it is still FGM.

Where does FGM take place?

FGM is a global problem. This means it is practised all over the world although some regions are more affected than others, for example, Asia, the Middle East and Africa (where it is practised in over 28 countries). It is estimated that worldwide, more than 200 million girls and women alive today have undergone female genital mutilation. Moreover, an estimated 3 million girls are said to be at risk of undergoing female genital mutilation every year.

When is FGM performed?

Although FGM is most commonly performed on girls between the ages of 5 and 8, it is also performed on babies, teenagers and even on adult women. People who campaign against FGM say that not all cases are reported and that the number of girls who are victims of it is rising. People who oppose FGM focus on human rights violations, lack of informed consent, and health risks. It is important to raise awareness of the practice of FGM and to inform young people of the facts and issues.

What are the health risks of FGM?

FGM can result in physical, emotional and psychological problems and in extreme cases, death. The health problems can be short-term (immediately after FGM is performed) and long-term (potentially for the rest of a girl's/woman's life).

Physical health problems include:

- Severe pain and/or shock during the procedure
- Severe blood loss during the procedure
- Increased risk of infections such as tetanus or HIV (especially in cases where the same instruments are used on a number of girls)
- Difficulties in passing urine
- Urinary tract infections
- Menstrual problems, which can include difficulties with blood flow due to the small hole left, excessively long and painful periods, and infections due to blood collecting inside the vagina and uterus
- Complications in pregnancy and or childbirth
- Pain or difficulty during sex

Psychological effects includes:

- Post-traumatic stress, which can include anger, flashbacks, nightmares, anxiety, and depression.
- Psycho-sexual problems (fear and difficulties in having sex)
- Feelings of not being a 'whole' or a 'normal' girl or woman.

Some girls or women may not experience all or any of the listed problems or they may not even be aware that these problems are related to FGM.

It is however important to note though that all types of FGM are harmful and violate girls' and women's human rights and serve no medical purpose.

Is FGM legal?

In not just Scotland but the whole of the UK, and many other countries, FGM is considered a human rights violation, a form of child abuse and a criminal offense. It is therefore illegal to perform, help, support or arrange for FGM to be carried out on someone in the UK. It is also illegal to take someone outside the UK to have FGM carried out. The offence can result in 14 years in prison or a fine or both. In 2017–2018 there were approximately 250 women identified with FGM after attending hospital in Scotland. This figure only shows those who have attended hospital and not how many women and girls live with FGM.

Activity 1

You are a radio journalist reporting on the news shown in Source 2 about an FGM prosecution in England, which you have just read in *The Guardian*. You need to re-write this article, reducing it to 150 words. The article needs to contain all the important facts.

THE NEWS

Mother of three-year-old convicted of FGM in UK

The mother of a three-year-old girl has become the first person to be found guilty of female genital mutilation (FGM) in the UK in a landmark case welcomed by campaigners.

The Ugandan woman, 37, and her Ghanaian partner, 43, both from Walthamstow, east London, were accused of cutting their daughter over the 2017 summer bank holiday.

While the parents were on bail, police searched the mother's home and found evidence of witchcraft, including spells aimed at silencing professionals involved in the case. Police found spells written inside 40 frozen limes and two ox tongues with screws embedded in them with the apparent aim of keeping police, social workers and lawyers quiet.

The mother cried in the dock as she was found guilty of FGM after the Old Bailey jury deliberated for less than a day. Her partner was cleared of all charges.

FGM was made illegal in the UK more than three decades ago but prosecutors have struggled to secure a conviction.

Lynette Woodrow, of the Crown Prosecution Service, said: "We can only imagine how much pain this vulnerable young girl suffered and how terrified she was. A three-year-old has no power to resist or fight back.

"Her mother then coached her to lie to the police so she wouldn't get caught but this ultimately failed. We will not hesitate to prosecute those who commit this sickening offence."

The National Police Chiefs' Council (NPCC) lead for FGM, Commander Ivan Balhatchet, said: "We have always been clear that prosecutions alone will not stop this abuse, however this guilty verdict sends a strong message that police will make every effort possible to pursue those committing this heinous crime."

The two defendants were jointly accused of subjecting the girl to FGM by "deliberate cutting with a sharp instrument" at her mother's home in the presence of her father. Medics raised the alarm when the girl was taken to Whipps Cross hospital in north London with severe bleeding and a surgeon concluded the child had been cut with a scalpel.

Charlotte Proudman, a leading barrister who specialises in FGM, told the Guardian: "The conviction is hugely significant, securing justice for the girl but also in sending a strong message that this crime will not be tolerated."

There are an estimated 137,000 women and girls living with FGM in England and Wales according to City University. The Home Office has identified women from countries including Somalia, Kenya, Ethiopia and Nigeria as most at risk.

There have been 298 FGM protection orders issued since they were first introduced in 2015 to safeguard those at risk.

Source 2 Adapted from *The Guardian*, 1 February 2019

What happened to Waris?

Waris had FGM carried out at the age of five. She had type 3 FGM, where her clitoris and vulva were removed and then the remaining skin or the outer lips were pulled and sewn together, leaving a small hole for urine and menstrual flow. Suffering pain and infection, she eventually ran away from home because her father wanted to marry her off to an older man. When she finally arrived in England, she became a successful model. She was able to have an operation to undo the stitches. She said it was wonderful to be able to urinate and to not have trouble with her periods. However, she can never experience the sexual pleasure of a clitoris. She is now a United Nations special ambassador for women's rights and has started her own foundation to raise awareness against female genital mutilation.

Where can I find out more?

FORWARD has a useful resource for young people covering the definition of and types of FGM, which can be found at:
www.forwarduk.org.uk/forward-publications/fgm-faqs-a-campaigners-guide-for-young-people/

Becoming a woman (part 2)

In spite of my anger over what has been done to me, I don't blame my parents. I love my mother and father. My mother had no say in my circumcision, because as a woman she is powerless to make decisions. She was simply doing to me what had been done to her, and what had been done to her mother and her mother's mother. And my father was completely ignorant of the suffering he was inflicting on me. He knew that in our society, if he wanted his daughter to marry, she must be circumcised or no man would have her. My parents were both victims of their upbringing and cultural practices that have continued unchanged for thousands of years. But just as we know today that we can avoid disease and death by vaccinations, we know that women are not animals in heat, and their loyalty has to be earned with trust and affection rather than barbaric rituals. The time has come to leave the old ways and suffering behind. I feel that God made my body perfect the way I was born. Then man robbed me, took away my power and left me a cripple. My womanhood was stolen. If God had wanted those body parts missing, why did he create them? I just pray that one day no woman will have to experience this pain. It will become a thing of the past and the world will be safe for all women. What a happy day that will be, and that's what I'm working towards. God-willing, it will happen.

Source 3 From *Desert Flower* by Waris Dirie

Activity 2

Why do you think FGM is still being carried out?

Activity 3

Scenario 1

Your friend has told you that they are going abroad to have 'something done' and they are scared.

What can you say to her? What can you do?

Scenario 2

Nala's parents want FGM to be carried out on her.

She doesn't want it. What can she do?

By the end of 8.8 you will:
- be able to demonstrate putting someone in the recovery position
- describe the key steps in administering CPR.

Starter

Here are three examples of when health and safety must be considered – for your protection and everyone else's:
- A group of your friends have a day out cycling.
- Your Scout group spends the day travelling the canal on a barge.
- You are signing up for a new app.

Come up with at least three safety rules to follow for one of these situations.

Activity 1

In pairs, discuss what you should be aware of before or as you make a call to 999. Be prepared to feed back to the class.

Health and safety rules apply in everyday life. You may already have learned about making an emergency call by dialing 999. You may need to get help as soon as possible but there are things you must always consider in an emergency situation.

Here's some more potentially life-saving information:

- If someone collapses and you know that they've taken pills or alcohol, tell the ambulance crew when they arrive.

- If someone else is calling 999 for help, you could try to put the person into the recovery position (see Source 1).

Activity 2

In pairs, practise putting each other in the recovery position.

1 Place the arm nearest you at a right angle to the person's body.

2 Bring the far arm across the person's chest and place the back of their hand against their cheek. Bend the person's far leg at the knee.

3 While keeping the person's hand pressed against their cheek, pull the knee towards you, rolling the person towards you and onto their side.

4 Stay with the person until help arrives.

Source 1

If you find someone who has collapsed, you will need to know what to do. If someone is having a cardiac arrest, doing CPR right away can really help a person's chance of survival.

Learn these CPR steps now so you know what to do if someone is experiencing a life-threatening emergency.

If a person stops breathing, his or her heartbeat will also stop. These CPR steps (chest compressions and rescue breaths) will help circulation and get oxygen into the body. Early use of a defibrillator, if one is available, can restart a heart with an abnormal rhythm.

> **What is CPR?**
> CPR stands for cardiopulmonary resuscitation.
>
> **What is a cardiac arrest?**
> A cardiac arrest is caused by an electrical problem in the heart. This electrical problem causes the heart to stop pumping blood around the body and to the brain.

First, open a person's airway to check if they are breathing (don't begin CPR if a patient is breathing normally). Check that there is nothing blocking the airway.

1 Make sure the patient is lying on their back on a firm surface. Kneel beside him or her and place the heel of your hand on the centre of the chest.

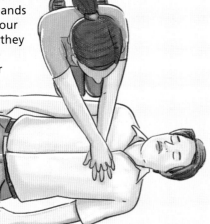

2 Keeping your arms straight, cover the first hand with the heel of your other hand and interlock the fingers of both hands together. Keep your fingers raised so they do not touch the patient's chest or rib cage.

Then, get help. If you are not alone, send someone to phone for help as soon as you have checked breathing and have the person confirm the call has been made. While help is on the way, follow these CPR steps:

3a Lean forward so that your shoulders are directly over the patient's chest and press down on the chest about two inches. Release the pressure, but not your hands, and let the chest come back up.

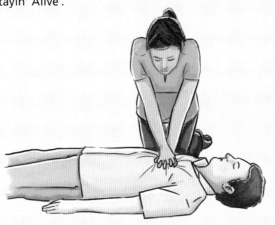

3b Repeat to give 30 compressions at a rate of 100 compressions per minute. Not sure what that really means? Push to beat of the Bee Gees song 'Stayin' Alive'.

Source 2 'Hands-only' CPR

115

Rescue breaths

If you just follow the steps so far, without rescue breaths, this is called 'Hands-Only CPR'. This is often recommended for people suffering out-of-hospital cardiac arrest because Hands-Only CPR might be more comfortable than doing rescue breaths for some bystanders (and so they might be more likely to take action!). But it's a good idea to learn how to give rescue breaths as you may need to administer CPR to a family member or a friend and you will want to give them the best possible chance of survival.

4 Move to the patient's head. Tilt his or her head and lift his chin to open the airway again. Let his or her mouth fall open slightly.

6 Remove your mouth from the patient's and look along the chest, watching the chest fall. Repeat steps five and six once more.

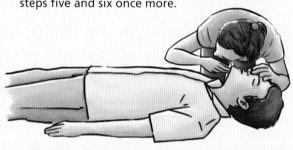

5 Pinch the nostrils closed with the hand that was on the forehead and support the patient's chin with your other hand. Take a normal breath, put your mouth over the patient's, and blow until you can see his or her chest rise.

7 Place your hands on the chest again and repeat the cycle of 30 chest compressions, followed by two rescue breaths.

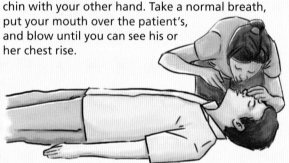

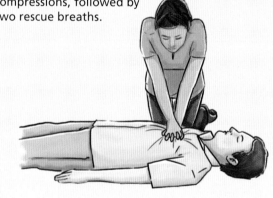

Source 3 'Rescue breaths' CPR

Activity 3

Encourage others to learn how to save a life. Design an infographic encouraging people to learn how to administer CPR.

Common injuries

Every year in the UK, thousands of people die or are seriously injured in incidents. Many deaths could be prevented if first aid was given before emergency services arrive.

Here are some of the most common injuries that may need emergency treatment in the UK:

- anaphylaxis (severe allergic reaction)
- bleeding heavily
- burns and scalds
- choking
- drowning
- fractures
- heart attack
- poisoning
- shock
- stroke

Remember: if someone is injured, you should:

- **first check that you and the casualty aren't in any danger, and, if possible, make the situation safe**
- **if necessary, dial 999 for an ambulance, when it's safe to do so**
- **carry out basic first aid.**

Source 4 First aid

Source 5 In an emergency, call 999 if the emergency services are required

Activity 4

Look at **www.firstaidchampions.redcross.org.uk/**.

In pairs, discuss at what age you think people should start learning first aid. Be prepared to feed back your answer and reasons to the class.

Note: This learning opportunity gives the basics on first aid and CPR, but remember it is recommended that everyone should go on a full first aid course, and wherever possible, seek the help of trained professionals and experts, or the emergency services.

8.9 Who can help?

By the end of 8.9 you will:
- be able to identify some sources of help and support
- have designed information for young people to use.

Starter

Where would you advise someone to look for information, help or support?

Work in pairs to identify where you could go for help if you were worried or concerned about yourself or another person's health, safety or wellbeing:
- in school
- in the local area
- using helplines or other media.

Remember to identify individuals who could help as well as organisations that might be useful.

Activity 1

1 Who would be your trusted person(s) to turn to for advice?
2 Why do you trust them?

Young people often have lots of questions that they would like help with. These questions may be about subjects such as emotions, relationships and money. They may also want information about exam stress or friendship problems. They might need help and support on some more specific issues like the ones we have looked at in this chapter.

Many young people know that the internet can also be a good source of advice and information.

Many websites provide information and support to young people.

Some websites are easier to use than others and the quality of information varies from site to site.

Source 1 www.childline.org.uk/. This is a national charity website that covers all sorts of issues that may affect young people.

Activity 2

Working in groups, your task is to look at a source of information for young people. You may be asked to look at one of the following websites:

www.childline.org.uk

www.youngscot.net

www.youngminds.org.uk

or another one that your teacher will give you.

Your task is to investigate it, sample how it works and produce a review to help others decide if it is a useful source of advice and help.

You will share your review with the rest of the class.

1 Your group should consider the following:
  a Was it easy to read?
  b Was it easy to navigate your way around the website and find more information?

c Was it interesting to look at?

d Would you recommend it as a source of help? Give examples to explain your responses.

2 Once your group has answered these questions, sum up your review of the website by giving it a score out of 10.

As a general guide:
- 3/10   Not very useful, hard to find information and so on
- 5/10   Average usefulness – worth a look
- 7/10   Has got some useful things in it but could be improved (say how)
- 10/10   Great advice, well presented

Activity 3

Design a poster or webpage that highlights some of the sources of information that got high marks in your class. On your poster it should be clear:
- what these sources of information are
- why they are useful
- where people can find them.

Your school may already have a 'help and information for students' noticeboard or section of its website. You could ask for your poster or webpage to be

displayed there. Remember that you will need to check with the students or staff who organise this noticeboard or part of the website to see if there are special requirements for displaying the information.

If your school doesn't have anything like this, then your year group could take on the task of asking your School/pupil Council (or other student organisation) to set one up.

- Knife crime
  www.noknivesbetterlives.com
- Bullying
  www.respectme.org.uk
  www.bullying.co.uk
- Female genital mutilation
  www.forwarduk.org.uk
  www.childline.org.uk/
  info-advice/bullying-abuse-
  safety/abuse-safety/female-
  circumcision-fgm-cutting/
- Internet safety
  www.thinkuknow.co.uk
  www.childnet.com
- Homelessness
  scotland.shelter.org.uk/
  get_advice/advice_topics/
  homelessness
- Protecting childhood
  www.nspcc.org.uk/what-
  we-do/policy-influencing/
  Scotland
  www.nspcc.org.uk
- Drug taking
  www.drugsand.me

Activity 4

Sometimes you may need more specific help. Search for the organisations in Source 2 when seeking help or advice – for yourself or other people.

Activity 5

Can you identify a new fact or a helping person/agency you hadn't heard of until today?

Source 2 Help agencies

9 Identity

9.1 Who am I?

By the end of 9.1 you will:
- **know what is meant by 'identity'**
- **be able to state some things that make up someone's identity.**

Starter

Look at Source 1. Where someone is from is an important part of their identity. How would these young people's identities be similar? How would these young people's identities be different? Discuss these questions in pairs. Be prepared to feed back to the class.

Source 1 Who are they?

Our identity is 'who we are'. It is what makes us, us!

Look around your classroom. In some ways you are all similar. Can you think of any examples? In some ways you are all different. Can you think of some examples? We are going to look at what things make up a person's identity.

Activity 1

Think of ten things about yourself. Jot them down if necessary but keep them hidden. Join with a partner who knows you quite well. See if they can guess these ten things. Then swap.

These ten things are the type of things that make up your identity.

Activity 2

When people talk about their identity they usually talk about friends, family, hobbies and interests, clubs, places, gender, faith and beliefs, race and cultures.

1 Did you think about these things?
2 What else did you think about?
3 How was your identity different to someone else's?

Reflect upon these questions. Share your thoughts with a partner.

Activity 4

Now, think about whether or not any of these things are worth anything to you:

- having a good friend
- being able to talk to a family member you trust
- the pleasure you get from having a pet
- finding time to watch TV or listen to music
- having the freedom to express your opinion.

When you hear the word 'value' you might think it simply means how much money something is worth. But the truth is we value all kinds of things in our lives, in lots of different ways. Most people have a range of values that influence the way they think, feel and behave. Some values will be more important to them than others.

Add some of the things you value to your 'Who am I?' identity circle so that it becomes an *identity and values circle*. Some things you value might be there already, like family and friends. You could add things like:

- living in a country where I will be able to vote
- knowing that people trust me to make decisions for myself
- having a choice of food to eat.

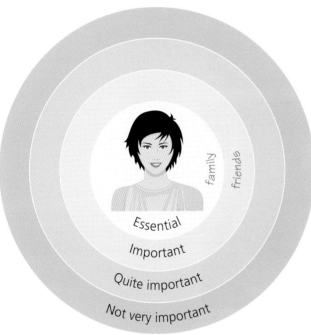

Source 2 Who am I?

Activity 5

In pairs, agree upon a definition for the word 'identity'. Be prepared to feed back to the class.

Activity 3

Look at Source 2. Draw and complete your own 'Who am I?' identity circle. Sketch a portrait of yourself in the middle. Think about what is essential to your identity; what is important; what is quite important and what is not very important.

By the end of 9.2 you will:
- be able to identify different types of families
- understand some of the roles and responsibilities of parents and carers with respect to raising children
- describe how family relationships can affect wellbeing.

Starter

Look at the photos in Source 1 and see if you can come up with some answers to these questions:
1. What do you think these families might have in common with each other?
2. Does a family always live together? Why might they live in different houses or places?
3. What makes a group of people a family?
4. How much is a young person influenced by their family?

Source 1 Different types of family

A coat of arms is a unique design painted on a shield. These designs used to be inherited, meaning that they were passed down within families. In the past, coats of arms were normally for real people but nowadays lots of countries and businesses also have coats of arms. Each symbol on the coat of arms will represent something that has an important meaning to that person, country or company.

Activity 1

Look at Source 2 which shows an imaginary coat of arms.

Design your own coat of arms. This might include an image of something that represents where you are from, for example, a flag, a national emblem or flower, a city logo or an image that represents the sea or hills. It could have something that represents your family, including pets.

Source 2 Coat of arms

Activity 2

No family is perfect and there are all sorts of things that family members can do to get on.

1 Read the speech bubbles in Source 3 to see what other young people have suggested.

2 In small groups, write a list of top tips for young people and adults who are living together as a family. Come up with at least five positive things that young people could do or say. Now find five things that adults could do or say. Think about why these are good examples and explain how they could help families to live in harmony. Here is an example:

Young people	Adults
I will walk the dog when it's my turn on the rota.	If you do what you agreed on the rota then I won't nag!

Don't be cheeky!

Try and get on – make compromises. That way you get somewhere.

Just be honest with your parents, because if you lie to them … well they know, and it doesn't really help.

My mum has a lot to cope with – the twins and me and my brother. But I do what I can to help, like washing up and stuff.

Just try not to fight with your brothers and sisters because that puts a strain on everything, especially your parents.

Source 3 Talking about families

Activity 3

What are the roles and responsibilities of parents and carers when raising children? Work in pairs and decide which of these are the responsibility of parents or carers and which are not!

- Making sure the kids are always happy.
- Bringing your children up to be independent.
- Keeping your children safe from harm.
- Giving your children everything they ask for.
- Teaching your kids to read and write.
- Being good role models for your children.
- Making sure your kids are not hungry and thirsty.
- Making sure your children are well-behaved.
- Ensuring your children attend school.
- Taking your children on holiday.

Activity 4

Some people who have known each other for a really long time sometimes say they feel 'part of the family'. Sometimes joining a club, an activity or a faith group can also give us a 'family' to which we can belong. Who would you bring together in your 'ideal family' household?

By the end of 9.3 you will:
- understand that both adults and children have roles and responsibilities within families
- have practised the social skill of appreciation within relationships.

Starter

Living together as a family involves everyone doing their share. Think of one thing that is your particular responsibility in your home, or a task that you always do. Explain what it is to your partner and whether you like doing it, or not!

Not everyone will like all the tasks that need to be done around the house. Should different members of a family have specific roles in the household? Look at how one family (where there are two adults and two children) share the various household responsibilities.

Task	Example family	
Cleaning the kitchen	Adult 1 helped by child 2 sometimes	
Cleaning the bathroom	Adult 2	
Cooking	Adult 1	
Doing the ironing	Adult 1 – sometimes other family members help out	
Tidying the living area(s)	Adult 1 and child 2	
Tidying bedroom(s)	Each does their own	
Looking after pets	Child 1	
Domestic shopping (food and cleaning products)	Adult 2	
Jobs outside the house: gardening, car washing	Adult 1 and child 1	

Source 1 Family life

It's not just sharing out the tasks that can cause problems in a family. There can be all sorts of reasons for family rows and upsets.

Look at the things in Source 2 that families find help their communal life to run more smoothly.

Activity 1

1 Draw up your own chart based on the tasks in Source 1.
List who carries out each task in *your* family.

2 Now get into groups. Think about how it was decided who would do each task in the first place and discuss the following questions in your group:

a Do you do any tasks? Why? Why not? Do you think you should?

b Did you choose your tasks, or were you told which tasks you had to do?

c Do you think the distribution of tasks in your family is fair?

d If you don't do your task, does another family member always end up doing it for you?

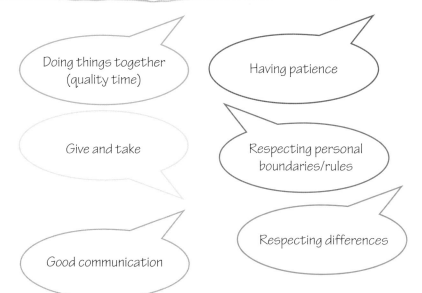

Doing things together (quality time)

Having patience

Respecting personal space

Give and take

Respecting personal boundaries/rules

Keeping a sense of humour

Good communication

Respecting differences

Showing affection

Source 2 Happy families?

Activity 2

1 Work together as a group and discuss the speech bubbles in Source 2. Construct a Diamond Nine by ranking each item in a diamond, like the one below.
2 The item that you think is most important should go at the top and the one you think is the least important should be at the bottom. Make sure you discuss why you have ranked them in that order.
3 There are nine items in the speech bubbles. If you had to add a tenth one, what would it be?

The statements in the Diamond Nine all describe positive ways of getting along with each other, but when living communally, we can sometimes take each other for granted. We might forget to thank a family member who helps us or whose company we really enjoy.

4 Think about the people you live with. Is there someone who you would like to thank?

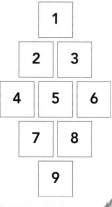

Thank you

for the way you do the things you do

Way to go!
Well done!!!

You are an inspiration

Source 3 Appreciation cards

Activity 3

1 Why might it sometimes be important to make the time to say thank you to the people who are around you every day?
2 Look at the cards in Source 3 to give you ideas to make an appreciation card or poem that you could give to someone whose contribution to your life you value.

Activity 4

What do you think your family members would say is the main contribution you make to family life?

125

9.4 Gender identity

By the end of 9.4 you will:

- be able to state what 'gender identity' means and give a range of terms to describe gender identity

Starter

In pairs, discuss the term 'gender' – what does it mean? What words have you heard to describe gender?

What is gender identity?

Gender identity is the personal sense of one's own gender. A person's gender identity might match the sex they were assigned at birth or it may not. People who do not identify with the sex they were assigned at birth are described as transgender. Transgender is an umbrella term for anyone who does not identify with the sex they were assigned at birth. There are a range of gender identities within the trans community including male, female, non-binary, and gender-fluid. There are many different terms to describe gender.

Trans male: A man or boy who was assigned female at birth.

Trans female: A woman or girl who was assigned male at birth.

Non-binary: Someone who does not identify entirely as male or female.

Gender-fluid: Someone whose gender identity can change over time.

Source 1 Transgender symbol

People whose gender matches the sex they were assigned at birth are described as cisgender. So, gender identity is how someone feels on the inside.

What is gender expression?

Gender expression is how someone presents themselves to the world, through how they look, dress or behave. People often make assumptions about someone's gender identity based on their appearance, but a person's gender expression may not match their gender identity.

Providing support

Activity 1

Read Source 2. Discuss with a partner what you think Charlie should do. What support is available for them? What could school do to support Charlie? On your own, write a letter from Charlie to their family explaining how they feel and what they need.

Activity 2

Discuss with a partner what makes a school community a safe place for individuals to express themselves and their gender identity. Be prepared to feed back.

Activity 3

In pairs, imagine you've been tasked with creating a noticeboard in school to get people thinking about gender identity and raising awareness of transgender people. What would you display on it? Create a plan of what you would include. Be prepared to present your ideas to the class.

Charlie is 11. Since primary school they have always felt different and like they didn't fit in with other children in the class. Now they've moved to secondary school it's got even worse. Recently Charlie read an article online about a pop star who is non-binary. Reading the article made everything make sense for Charlie. This is who they are. Just like the pop star, they don't feel male or female, they are non-binary. Charlie doesn't know how to tell their parents or who to turn to for support.

Source 2 Charlie

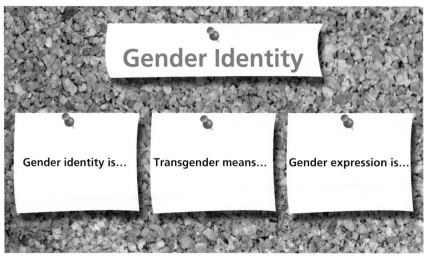

Source 3 Creating a noticeboard

By the end of 9.5 you will:

- be aware of the negative consequences of stereotypes and prejudice

Starter

In pairs, discuss what you understand by the word 'stereotype'. Make a list of any stereotypes that you have heard.

The pictures shown in Source 1 are from a film and stage musical called *Billy Elliot*. Billy was a boy who had a passion and a gift for ballet, but he was told by his dad that he couldn't do it because it was 'for girls'. Despite his dad's negativity, Billy pursued his passion and became a successful ballet dancer dancing in *Swan Lake*.

Activity 1

Look at Source 1. *Billy Elliot* was set in the 1980s. Back then, gender stereotypes were more common. It was quite normal for people to have set opinions about what people of different genders could or couldn't do.

1   Discuss with your partner: How much do you feel that attitudes have changed since the 1980s? Could this situation still happen today?
2   Think back to the stereotypes you discussed at the beginning. Were any of these stereotypes around gender?
3   In pairs, imagine Billy had listened to his dad and hadn't pursued his passion; what would the impact have been on Billy?

Source 1 Scenes from the film and stage musical of *Billy Elliot*

How would you define or explain 'stereotypes'?

Stereotypes: that's thinking all people who belong to a certain group are the same and labelling them, for example, 'all young people who wear hoodies are thugs'.

How would you define or explain 'prejudice'?

Prejudice: that's when you judge someone without knowing them, on the basis of what they look like or what group they belong to, and then behave in a certain way towards them.

How can stereotyping encourage prejudice?

Well, let's think … How do you think some adults, society and the media label teenagers who wear hoodies? Perhaps they consider them to be thugs

What prejudiced attitudes or behaviour could this lead to?

Well, some young people could be excluded from something or somewhere because they are thought of as thugs.

Is that fair?

Some perhaps may be thugs but most won't be, but they are all being judged to be the same.

Source 2 Stereotypes and prejudice

Activity 2

In pairs, read and discuss Source 2 which explores the link between stereotypes and how they might encourage prejudice. Choose three of the stereotypes that you discussed in the starter activity. If somebody held these views what prejudiced attitudes or behaviour (discrimination) could this lead to?

Activity 3

The Equality Act 2010 protects people from discrimination. There are nine personal characteristics that are protected by the Equality Act – can you name them? Discuss as a class.

Activity 4

Can you think of any modern-day examples where someone's actions have actively challenged a widely-held stereotype?

The Equality Act
In order to protect people from discrimination, the UK introduced the Equality Act 2010. This protects people from discrimination in employment, public services and in wider society. Those who experience discrimination can use the law to take action against those who have discriminated against them.

By the end of 9.6 you will:
- be able to describe what 'faith' and 'values' are and where they come from
- be able to say what values you hold.

Starter

Imagine someone says:

> I value planet Earth and have concerns about climate change – so I do my best to support organisations that stop the destruction of the rainforests. For example, I only use recycled paper.

This person has a value that affects the way they behave. What value or values do you hold that make you act in a certain way?

Activity 1

1 What is 'faith'?
2 What does it mean to have faith in someone?
3 Make a list of people you trust and believe in. Against each name make a note of why you believe and trust in that person.
4 Why is it important to believe in people and trust these people? Explain your answer.

Faith

Charles Blondin was a man who believed in himself. He was a famous tightrope walker. In 1859 he walked on a tightrope across Niagara Falls (335 metres). He made the return trip pushing a wheelbarrow, then did it twice more carrying his friend on his back. He asked the crowd, 'Do you believe I can do it again?' They all shouted 'Yes!' He said, 'Well, get in the barrow and I will take you.' Everyone refused. They all failed to trust him. The crowd believed he could do it but did not trust him with their own lives. They did not have faith in him.

Source 1 The Story of Charles Blondin

To have faith means to trust and believe in someone or something. Faith requires belief and trust.

Faith is about what you personally believe. It exists (or not) independently of whether or not you ever tell anyone about your beliefs and independently of whether or not anyone else shares your beliefs.

Religion is organised faith. A group of people with similar faith that in some manner share their faith is a religion. Religion is interrelated with race, ethnicity and culture.

Activity 2

By now you will have a clearer idea of some of the things you value. This activity asks you to think about the bigger picture.

1 Look at the values listed below:
   a Being free to express our opinions
   b Enjoying ourselves
   c Having human rights
   d Feeling safe
   e Having rules and laws
   f Being free to have our own beliefs
   g Having good health services
   h Having respect
   i Being trusted

   These are the values we often share in our communities and the society in which we live. Which of the values is most important to you?

2 Look at Source 2. It shows a Diamond Nine arrangement for placing your values in a priority order. Sort the nine values listed above, placing the one of most value to you in position 1 and the one of least value in position 9.

3 Consider the nine values listed above and your own values that you identified in the Starter Activity. If you could only choose one to have in your life, what would your most prized value be – and why?

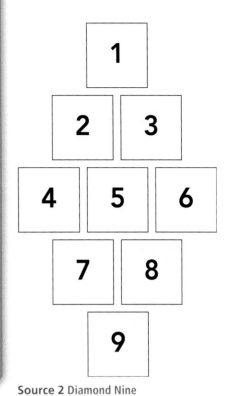

Source 2 Diamond Nine

Activity 3

Look at the items below.

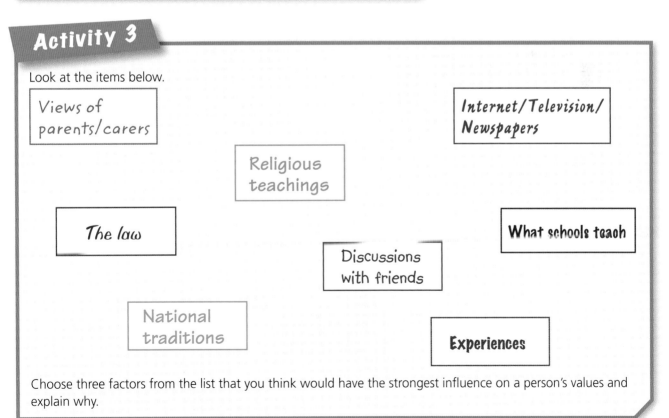

Views of parents/carers

Internet/Television/Newspapers

Religious teachings

The law

What schools teach

Discussions with friends

National traditions

Experiences

Choose three factors from the list that you think would have the strongest influence on a person's values and explain why.

Values

Having different values from others is something we discover as we get older and meet an increasingly wider variety of people outside our own circle of family and close friends. Values should influence the way we meet, work and live with others.

1 Food: not eating meat or animal products is better for both the environment and people's health.

2 Relationships: parents or carers should be able to approve whoever you go out with.

3 Community: senior citizens should always move to the front of the queue.

Source 3 Value statements

Case study

Greta Thunberg initiated the school strike for climate movement that formed in November 2018. She became a role model for worldwide student activism. The 17 United Nations Sustainable Development Goals (SDGs) are a universal call to action to end poverty, protect the planet and ensure that all people enjoy peace and prosperity. The UN SDG #13 is Climate Action.

Activity 5

1 What values did Greta use to influence her work and interactions with others?
2 Your teacher will put you into groups and suggest a value for your group to work with. Discuss how this value would influence Greta's work. Be prepared to feed back to the class.

Source 4 Changemakers

Can you think of any other famous people who have helped to change the world for the better? What did they do?

Activity 6

Look at Source 4. All of these people can be called 'Changemakers'. Can you name them? What contribution have they made to the world?

Activity 7

1 What things do you value for yourself? (Examples may include being honest or kind.)
2 What things do you value for other people? (These are things that may not apply in your life but which you can see have value for others. For example, you may not like sport but can see how being a good sportsperson might be important to others.)

Activity 8

Reflect upon how faith and values shape someone's identity.

By the end of 9.7 you will:
- be able to say what you have accomplished
- be able to recognise your own skills, qualities and achievements
- have practised the skill of appreciation.

Starter

It is important that children and young people have a big say in the decisions that affect them. The personal and social education that you have received will have helped you to learn about things that are important in your lives and how these things can affect you.

Working in groups, think back over what you have covered in PSE and see if you can agree on one key thing that:

a   you have learned that was new to all of you
b   you would like to learn more about
c   enabled you to practise a useful skill.

Activity 1

1   If you could choose your own personal qualities, for example, being friendly, cheerful, adventurous or sensitive, what would you choose? Take a few minutes to think about this and come up with three qualities that you would like to have.

Now that you've had the chance to think about the qualities you *wish* you had, here's an opportunity to hear about the positive qualities your classmates *know* you have.

2   In your group, look at Source 1. Select examples of the positive qualities that you see in each other. Give your reasons for selecting these qualities – and invent extra ones if you wish.

tries hard	likeable	confident	quiet	friendly	careful	sociable	loyal
thoughtful	warm-hearted	considerate	trustworthy	generous	kind		
humorous	responsible	honest	popular	cheerful	good listener		
brave	fair	intelligent	polite	bright	reasonable	helpful	capable
great sense of humour	laid back	tolerant	reliable	amiable	tenacious		
calm	considerate	fun	sensible	happy	hard-working		

Source 1 Positive qualities

Activity 2

Work as a group of three. The image of the tree in Source 2 depicts a person's good qualities, the skills they have developed and some of their short-term goals. Think about how you will complete your tree to 'symbolise' you. Discuss your trees to help each other decide what you would put on them.

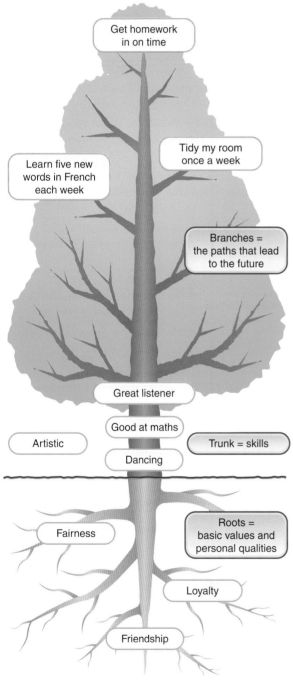

Source 2 The tree of me

Get homework
in on time

Tidy my room
once a week

Learn five new
words in French
each week

Branches =
the paths that lead
to the future

Great listener

Good at maths

Artistic

Trunk = skills

Dancing

Fairness

Roots =
basic values and
personal qualities

Loyalty

Friendship

Activity 3

Working as a group of six, fill in 'affirmations' for the other members of your group. Draw five leaves on a piece of paper, write down the name of each person in your group on a leaf, then write one thing that you really appreciate about them. Then cut out the leaves and hand them in; your contributions will be anonymous.

Activity 4

You will be given the five leaves with your name on that were completed in Activity 3. Read these and then complete this sentence:

I appreciate all the leaves I received, the one I'd like to share is … because …

By the end of 9.8 you will:

- understand that people have rights regardless of their different race, religion, culture, ability or disability, gender, age or sexual orientation
- be able to state some of the rights that apply to you as a young person
- understand that every right comes with its own responsibility.

Starter

Why have people needed to make rules and laws to protect their rights as human beings? (Clue – think about freedom, protecting life and so on.) Can you think of any examples of laws that were made specifically to protect children and young people?

Activity 1

The government often makes new laws and old laws are frequently amended. You may have learned about various laws, called 'Acts', during PSE or other subjects. Sometimes when you have learned about a law, you are given its date and told it has since been amended. For example, the 'Misuse of Drugs Act 1971 (and subsequent amendments)'. There are laws and rules to make sure that you and others are not discriminated against, like the Equality Act 2010.

Only a short time ago all decisions in some schools were made by adults alone – there were no School or Pupil Councils or other ways that students could voice their opinions.

When and where are there chances for you to get involved in rule-making in your school?

Article 12
Children have the right to say what they think should happen, when adults are making decisions that affect them, and to have their opinions taken into account.

Article 15
Children have the right to meet together and to join groups and organisations, as long as this does not stop other people from enjoying their rights.

Article 17
Children have the right to reliable information from the mass media. Television, radio, and newspapers should provide information that children can understand, and should not promote materials that could harm children.

Source 1 UN rights

Activity 2

Look at the three rights that young people have in Source 1. These come from The United Nations Convention on the Rights of the Child. These rights are called 'Articles'. The United Kingdom has signed up to this Convention so they are your rights too.

Work in pairs to discuss one of these Articles. Come up with answers for these questions:

1 Do you think you and your friends get a real chance to exercise this right?
2 What might get in the way, or stop you fully benefiting from this right?
3 What do you think would have to change to make this right apply 100 per cent in your life?

Source 2 The United Nations headquarters in New York

You might want to research more information on the Convention of the Rights of the Child – there are 54 Articles!

Rights are extremely important. Without them we might have no education, be sent out to work for very low wages, work very long hours, have no freedom to choose what we could watch on TV or access on the internet.

So it's important to protect rights. One way of doing this is to remember that every right comes with a responsibility. Each person needs to get involved in protecting their rights and being responsible for other people's rights.

If children have a **right** to be protected from conflict, cruelty, exploitation and neglect, then they also have a **responsibility** not to bully or harm each other.

If children have a **right** to a clean environment, then they also have a **responsibility** to do what they can to look after their environment.

If children have a **right** to be educated, then they have the **obligation** to learn as much as their capabilities allow and, where possible, share their knowledge and experience with others.

Source 3 UN responsibilities

Activity 3

If you were a member of your School or Pupil Council, how would you ensure that the responsibilities in Source 3 were taken on by the students in your school?

Activity 4

How would you complete these sentences?

- *As I get older I think an important right in my life will be …*
- *I will balance this right with taking responsibility for …*

By the end of 10.1 you will:

- understand that there are different groups in our communities
- identify similarities and differences between yourself, your classmates and others
- be able to state how you are unique.

Starter

Think of a word that describes you – the word must begin with the first letter of your first name, for example: 'I am Happy Halle' or 'I am Talented Toby'.

Activity 1

Look at the photos in Source 1 and the information in Source 2. These photographs represent some of the variety of people in Britain today. Think about how you would answer these questions:

1 Were any people in the images familiar to you in any way? Did you recognise national or religious clothing, symbols, and so on?
2 What differences/similarities did you notice?
3 What do all these people have in common?

Source 1 A selection of people in Britain today

In Britain people are protected from discrimination in different ways.

You should not be discriminated against in employment or in the services you receive because:

- of your race
- of your religious beliefs
- of your sexual orientation
- of your age (that you are 'too' young or 'too' old)
- of your gender
- of gender reassignment
- you are married or in a partnership
- you have a disability
- you are pregnant.

Source 2 The personal characteristics listed in the Equality Act

Activity 2

You are going to prepare to interview your partner. First you will need to come up with a list of questions. This will cover a variety of likes and dislikes, such as favourite TV programmes, favourite food, pet or no pet, favourite pop group, and so on. Some examples are shown below:

✓ What are your likes?

✓ What are your dislikes?

✓ What are your favourite TV programmes?

✓ What is your favourite food?

✓ What music do you like?

Now, interview your partner.

Once you have your answers, reflect upon the special things about your partner that make them unique. What positive things can you find about your partner that make them unique?

Now write a paragraph about your partner so that you can introduce them to others.

Activity 3

You will probably have learned a lot about several people in your class today. Now think about some things you have learned about yourself during this activity.

What made you feel you are unique?

By the end of 10.2 you will:
- be able to reflect on 'difference' and what it means to individual people
- be able to explain how prejudice might be challenged.

Source 1 Difference

Starter

Look at Source 1. What do the photographs tell us about 'difference'?

We all know what it feels like to be different in one way or another. We may know how uncomfortable and hurtful it can be if we are made to feel inferior because of that difference.

In the worst cases a fear and hatred of people who are different has led to events such as the Holocaust in the Second World War, 'ethnic cleansing' in the former Yugoslavia (1992), the genocide in Rwanda (1994), the humanitarian crisis in Darfur in the Sudan (2003), and 'ethnic cleansing' in the Afrin region of Syria (2017).

Recognising, understanding and accepting that there will always be similarities and differences between people may prevent ignorance, prejudice and fear from flourishing in the world.

Ethnic cleansing is the forced removal of ethnic, racial and/or religious groups from a place by a more (economically, politically, militarily) powerful ethnic group. This often leaves a remaining population of just one ethnicity.

Genocide is the mass extermination of a whole group of people in an attempt to wipe them out of existence.

Carmel

I liked my old school, but not my new school. In my old school I had lots of friends who were also black; in this school there are hardly any black people and none in my class. In learning opportunities I feel OK, but I worry about break and dinner time when I find it difficult to find someone to hang out with. Everyone seems to have their own friendship groups and I am not included. This is supposed to be a better school, but I don't like it and I want to go back to my old school.

Carmel is a young black woman.

Daniel

It was easy for me not to go to school. Mum and Dad worked and I often left the house after them and got back before them. They didn't know I wasn't going to school. I didn't do homework; the boys would take my bag off me when I got to school and throw the books about. When I didn't have my homework I couldn't tell the teacher it had been thrown away so I got into more trouble. It was better to stay at home.

Daniel has a learning disability.

Peter

Whenever people ridiculed somebody or something they called it 'gay'; people's trainers, music – even pencils – got called 'gay'. And there was nothing in school that showed positive images of gay people ... and there was no discussion about some people being gay and therefore I felt isolated. I didn't feel that I fitted in.

Peter is a young gay man.

Source 2 Feeling different

Activity 1

Read the three case studies in Source 2 and, in pairs, discuss the following questions about one of them.

1 How would you feel if this happened to you?
2 Do you think the person in the case study has any options, other than avoiding people? What are those options?
3 Is there any helpful advice you could give them?

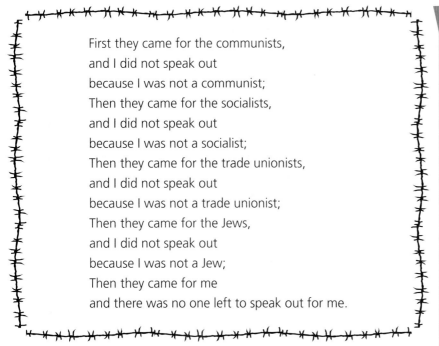

First they came for the communists,
and I did not speak out
because I was not a communist;
Then they came for the socialists,
and I did not speak out
because I was not a socialist;
Then they came for the trade unionists,
and I did not speak out
because I was not a trade unionist;
Then they came for the Jews,
and I did not speak out
because I was not a Jew;
Then they came for me
and there was no one left to speak out for me.

Source 3 Not speaking out: A famous poem urging people to speak out against prejudice. It is attributed to Martin Niemöller, a prominent anti-Nazi German pastor.

Activity 2

Read the poem in Source 3. It is a famous poem urging people to speak out against prejudice. It is attributed to Martin Niemöller, a prominent anti-Nazi German pastor. In speaking out against prejudice and hatred, he was trying to make an important point. Answer the following questions:

1 What do you think is the central message of the poem?
2 Who are the 'they' mentioned in the poem?
3 What does the poem have to do with our lives at school?
4 Why is it important to defend other people's rights?

Activity 3

Rewrite the poem in Source 3 in the context of today. What groups of people do you feel could be included now?

As individuals we each value different things. Former President of the US, Barack Obama, spoke about our common values. He said, 'the call to love one another; to understand one another; to treat with dignity and respect those with whom we share a brief moment on this Earth is the golden rule.'

Activity 4

What golden rule could you make that would express your values towards other people?

By the end of 10.3 you will:
- be able to talk about the communities that you belong to
- be able to recognise similarities and differences between yourself and others
- value the similarities between people.

Starter

Your teacher will ask you to go and stand in a range of varying groups. Did anyone stay in the same group? It is important to remember that we are all different in many ways but that we also share things.

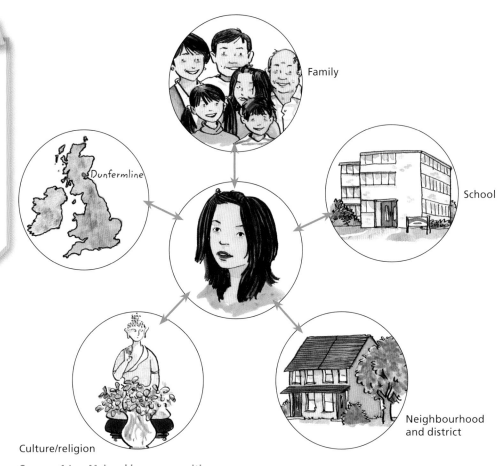

Source 1 Lee Mei and her communities

Source 1 depicts Lee Mei. She is a thirteen-year-old girl. As you can see, she belongs to a variety of communities:

- She is a member of the Lee family. (In Chinese culture the family name comes before the given (first) name.)
- She is a member of Second Year (S2) at her local secondary school.
- She lives in a semi-detached house in the Garvock area of Dunfermline.
- She and her mum, dad, grandfather, sister and brother are Buddhists.
- She is a British citizen and has a United Kingdom passport.

Sir Chris Hoy, multiple Olympic gold medalist for cycling. He was appointed a KBE in 2009

Dame Katherine Grainger, multiple Olympic medalist for rowing. She was appointed a DBE in 2017.

Source 2 Sports people awarded knighthoods (KBE and DBE)

Even though people live their lives in different types of communities, we all share similar experiences. For example, everyone has a birthday (whether or not they celebrate it); people have favourite or special foods; most people enjoy some kind of community celebration once a year; people mark special stages in their lives with parties and ceremonies and so on.

Source 2 is an example of individual people who, although they may appear 'different', actually share important similarities with each other.

Activity 1

Everyone belongs to more than one community. Draw a diagram either like Lee Mei's in Source 1 or of your own design to represent you and the different communities to which you belong.

Activity 2

Look at Source 2. These pictures show two Scottish sports people who have been awarded high honours (KBE and DBE). Can you think of other ways in which people, who appear different at first glance, may share similarities?

What are the differences or similarities between a KBE and a DBE?

Activity 3

Work together in a small group and discuss the following topics – see if you share any similarities across the whole group.
- One activity that you all enjoy.
- One healthy food that you all enjoy eating.
- One achievement you've all experienced since joining this school.
- One badge/charity bracelet that you would all be proud to wear.

Activity 4

There are many things that humans have in common: a range of emotions and the desire to be with others, but what makes us different from each other? Complete this sentence:

I share … with the entire human race and I am also unique and special because …

By the end of 10.4 you will:

- be able to identify the communities you belong to
- be able to suggest some guidelines for successful community life
- understand what qualities improve community life.

Starter

We each belong to a number of communities, for example, our neighbourhood; our family; our school; perhaps a religious or cultural community; and we are all citizens of larger communities such as our country Scotland, and the United Kingdom.

Name four communities that you belong to and, for each one, identify something you enjoy or benefit from by being part of that community.

Source 1 Looking after the community

Think back over your PSE course, and possibly other subjects too: you may have negotiated a Group Agreement based on rights and responsibilities. This was a type of 'community contract' where you gained rights and at the same time contributed by taking on responsibilities.

Activity 1

Source 1 shows individuals looking after their community. Each of us individually gains from being part of a community – and there are things we already do (or should be doing) so that other members of the community benefit as well. Take one of your example communities from the Starter activity and list three things you gain from being part of that community and three things you contribute to it.

Imagine a futuristic experiment which involves setting up a colony of people on a new planet (Novo-Earth, see Source 2). A representative selection of people from across the world has been chosen to take part in this new community. They include people with the variety of skills needed to set up a society, for example, teachers, doctors, engineers and so on. You are among the teenagers included. Everyone has a vital role to play and has been chosen because they are able to contribute to this new community.

The people of Novo-Earth will need to set up rules and guidelines to live by. Although these people come from many different countries on Earth, they all share Earth's Universal Declaration of Human Rights. As part of the consultation process you have been invited to put forward three rules or guidelines that uphold some of the Human Rights in the Declaration.

Source 2 Life in the new community of Novo-Earth

Activity 2

1 In groups, work on one of the categories below:
  - Education
  - Health and wellbeing
  - Equality
  - Employment
  - Freedom of thought/belief
2 Read the text on pages 146–147: The Universal Declaration of Human Rights: selected Articles.
3 For your allocated category, use your own words to explain three rules or guidelines for Novo-Earth that you think uphold some of the relevant points in the Universal Declaration of Human Rights.
4 Give feedback on your three points to the rest of the class.
5 Individually decide on which of the points in each category is the most important and take a class vote to decide the top guideline in each category. This should give you five key rules/guidelines for the new community.

Activity 3

Look back at Source 1. Leaving laws and guidelines aside, what ways of behaving would you like to see that would promote harmony and wellbeing?

Not all of the rules we live by are written down. Culturally, many groups have evolved informal ways of behaving that encourage harmony, for example, being courteous, respecting people who are different, helping neighbours, and so on.

Source 3 The United Nations represents the global community

Activity 4

Sometimes people talk about living by their 'golden rule', for example, 'Treat other people as you would like to be treated'. Communities could benefit from a golden rule too. What would be your golden rule for a *community* to live by and why?

The Universal Declaration of Human Rights: selected Articles

Article 1

All human beings are born free and equal in dignity and rights. They are endowed with reason and conscience and should act towards one another in a spirit of brotherhood.

Article 2

Everyone is entitled to all the rights and freedoms set forth in this Declaration, without distinction of any kind, such as race, colour, sex, language, religion, political or other opinion, national or social origin, property, birth or other status.

Article 3

Everyone has the right to life, liberty and security of person.

Article 4

No one shall be held in slavery or servitude; slavery and the slave trade shall be prohibited in all their forms.

Article 5

No one shall be subjected to torture or to cruel, inhuman or degrading treatment or punishment.

Article 6

Everyone has the right to recognition everywhere as a person before the law.

Article 7

All are equal before the law and are entitled without any discrimination to equal protection of the law.

Article 8

Everyone has the right to an effective remedy by the competent national tribunals for acts violating the fundamental rights granted him by the constitution or by law.

Article 9

No one shall be subjected to arbitrary arrest, detention or exile.

Article 10

Everyone is entitled in full equality to a fair and public hearing by an independent and impartial tribunal, in the determination of his rights and obligations and of any criminal charge against him.

Article 11

Everyone charged with a penal offence has the right to be presumed innocent until proved guilty according to law in a public trial at which he has had all the guarantees necessary for his defence.

Article 12

No one shall be subjected to arbitrary interference with his privacy, family, home or correspondence, nor to attacks upon his honour and reputation. Everyone has the right to the protection of the law against such interference or attacks.

Article 13

(1) Everyone has the right to freedom of movement and residence within the borders of each state.

(2) Everyone has the right to leave any country, including his own, and to return to his country.

Article 14

Everyone has the right to seek and to enjoy in other countries asylum from persecution.

Article 15

Everyone has the right to a nationality.

Article 16

Men and women of full age, without any limitation due to race, nationality or religion, have the right to marry and to found a family.

Article 17

Everyone has the right to own property alone as well as in association with others.

Article 18

Everyone has the right to freedom of thought, conscience and religion.

Article 19

Everyone has the right to freedom of opinion and expression.

Article 20

Everyone has the right to freedom of peaceful assembly and association.

Article 21

(1) Everyone has the right to take part in the government of his country, directly or through freely chosen representatives.

(2) Everyone has the right of equal access to public service in his country.

Article 22

Everyone, as a member of society, has a right to social security.

Article 23

(1) Everyone has the right to work, to free choice of employment, to just and favourable conditions of work and to protection against unemployment.

(2) Everyone, without any discrimination, has the right to equal pay for equal work.

(3) Everyone who works has the right to just and favourable remuneration.

(4) Everyone has the right to form and to join trade unions for the protection of his interests.

Article 24

Everyone has the right to rest and leisure, including reasonable limitation of working hours and periodic holidays with pay.

Article 25

Everyone has the right to a standard of living adequate for the health and wellbeing of himself and of his family, including food, clothing, housing and medical care and necessary social services, and the right to security in the event of unemployment, sickness, disability, widowhood, old age or other lack of livelihood in circumstances beyond his control.

Article 26

Everyone has the right to education.

Article 27

(1) Everyone has the right to freely participate in the cultural life of the community, to enjoy the arts and to share in scientific advancement and its benefits.

(2) Everyone has the right to the protection of the moral and material interests resulting from any scientific, literary or artistic production of which he is the author.

Article 28

Everyone is entitled to a social and international order in which the rights and freedoms set forth in this Declaration can be fully realised.

By the end of 10.5 you will:

- be able to consider problems from more than one point of view
- understand the importance of talking and negotiating in solving problems
- be able to describe the role of mediation in problem-solving.

Starter

Most people live happily together in their communities but sometimes things go wrong. What sorts of problems can arise between people who live in the same community?

The problems that arise in communities may often have more than one cause. There may be a particular incident or problem that has cropped up but also people's underlying feelings can make a situation more difficult. For example, if people feel angry, frightened or threatened they may respond in a way that makes the situation worse.

Source 1 Hanging out together

Activity 1

Look at the photograph in Source 1. It shows a group of young people who regularly gather together on one of the streets of a residential neighbourhood. Several residents are unhappy about the young people meeting like this.

1 What do you think the residents are concerned about?
2 What feelings might the residents have that could make the situation flare up?
3 How do you think a resolution might be reached?

Activity 2

Look at the situations described in Source 2. Working in groups, answer the following questions for one of the situations:

1 What reasonable point could either side raise to explain their concerns?
2 What feelings might each side be experiencing?
3 What negotiations and compromises would be necessary for the characters to achieve an outcome where both feel happier?

Anna

You are an enthusiastic amateur gardener keen on self-sufficiency and 'green' issues. You rented an allotment earlier this year and are growing your own fruit and veg. You won't use weedkiller and you work hard to keep your patch clear of weeds. You enjoy the friendly atmosphere between the different allotment holders and look forward to your weekly visits. However, you are concerned that George's weeds are creeping into your plot and killing your plants.

George

Your allotment is next to Anna's. You've had it for years and don't worry too much about weeds and creepers – as long as you can grow flowers and a few seasonal vegetables to take home to the family you are happy. Recently you haven't been able to visit as often as you'd like since your back has started playing up. Things are getting a bit out of hand on your allotment but you don't consider it a big problem.

Jay

You are fourteen years old and your parents have split up. You are happy at your present school and have lots of friends there. Your dad and his new partner have moved to the next town – about five miles away. Your mum is staying in the house where you all lived together and wants you to live with her. Your school is half way between the two homes so whatever happens you won't need to move schools. You'd like to spend your time equally with both parents – but they're angry with each other and won't discuss things.

Jon

You are Jay's father. You and your wife have split up after being together for sixteen years. You have had to move out of the home you all shared. You really miss Jay and would like it if Jay came to live with you. You feel really upset about the situation. Your ex-wife is angry with you and won't allow you back in the house. She completely blames you for the breakdown of the relationship. She doesn't want to speak to you.

Source 2 Problems, problems, problems

Mediation

One way that community or family disputes can be resolved is by a process called mediation. You may already have come across student mediation services in school, which sometimes deal with issues such as bullying. Here are just three examples of services that can help provide advice and/or mediation when things go wrong:

- Some local councils have a mediation service to resolve disputes between neighbours.

- The Citizens Advice Bureau can provide useful advice to anyone with a problem.

- Independent mediation services or charities are often used by families who are experiencing problems.

Activity 3

Look at the information in Source 3. Discuss what situations in school and your other communities might be helped if mediation was available.

What is mediation?

Mediation is used when people have a dispute (disagreement). It helps them to reach an agreement for the future which everyone is happy with. When mediation is used, people are not judged or blamed. It is a good way of making sure that everyone hears and understands all the issues that are involved.

How does mediation work?

The mediators will listen to what each person has to say and help them to explore the options available. The mediator will not tell the people what to do but will help them to reach an agreement.

Source 3 Mediation

By the end of 10.6 you will:
- be able to define hate incidents and hate crime
- describe the potential consequences for people convicted of hate crime
- understand what is meant by 'radicalisation'.

Starter

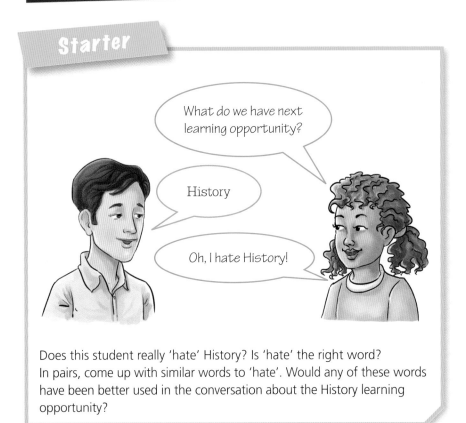

Does this student really 'hate' History? Is 'hate' the right word?
In pairs, come up with similar words to 'hate'. Would any of these words have been better used in the conversation about the History learning opportunity?

A crime is called a **hate crime** when it is motivated (encouraged) by hate. For instance, people who commit hate crimes target victims because they are or appear to hold a personal characteristic such as:

- race
- sex
- religion
- sexual orientation
- class
- age
- disability

Hate incidents include physical assault, destruction of property, bullying, harassment, verbal abuse or insults, or offensive graffiti or letters (often called hate mail). This also includes bullying, harassment and abuse via social media or online.

Being a victim of hate crime can leave a person frightened, isolated and vulnerable and can severely undermine their sense of safety. It impacts greatly on self-confidence and self-esteem and can lead to depression, anxiety and, in extreme cases, suicide. Therefore, when an offender (someone who has committed a crime) has been found guilty or pleaded guilty and the court is deciding on a sentence to be imposed, it must treat evidence of prejudice as something more serious. The court must state that fact openly so that everyone knows that the offence is being treated more seriously because of this evidence of prejudice.

It's important to remember:

- Any criminal conviction will have an impact on future life choices: there are some jobs, like working in a school, that you cannot do if you have been convicted of a crime.
- Criminal convictions must be declared to all potential employers if details are asked for.
- Hate crime has an impact on the lives of the victims but will also impact on the person carrying out the crime.
- Hate crime carries a more severe sentence than other similar crimes.

Activity 1

Based on what you have read so far, decide whether or not each of the incidents below is a hate crime, or just a regular criminal offence:

A Sarah is from a Muslim family. She wears a hijab when out in public, as do her mum and sisters. The word 'hijab' describes the act of covering up generally but is often used to describe headscarves worn by Muslim women. The scarf usually covers the head and neck but leaves the face clear. Recently, the family had anti-Muslim slogans graffitied on their house but they haven't suffered any physical violence.

B Stephen owns the village shop. He is involved in a lot of community work, helping refugees and asylum seekers. Last month, his car was stolen by thieves who had never met Stephen before and didn't know he was the owner of the car.

C Mark has Down syndrome. Mark and his brother were walking through the park when some teenagers filmed them on their phones. The teenagers uploaded the clip to YouTube. Other people posted abusive comments on YouTube, calling Mark derogatory names.

D Aisha, who is mixed race, was mugged on her way home from work. The mugger took her phone and purse and swore at her, using an insulting word for 'woman'.

E Sonny is part of a gypsy/traveller community who have recently moved onto a field on the outskirts of a town. Many people in the town are angry about the presence of the gypsy/traveller community, and some have started throwing rocks at the caravan windows. Sonny came home to find that his caravan had been broken into and someone had smashed up his personal property. His neighbour saw the criminals and knows they were part of the same group that have been throwing rocks.

F Lena came to Scotland from Poland three months ago to find work. She managed to find a job as a waitress but a few customers were upset that a Polish person was working in their café and have written letters of complaint to her manager asking for her to be sacked. Some of the letters were very abusive and used offensive language about Lena.

G Callum is 15 and has lots of friends who are girls but has never had a girlfriend. A group of students at school have been calling him names because they think he is gay. They have threatened to beat Callum up on his way home from school.

What is radicalisation?

Radicalisation is when someone starts to believe or support extreme views. They could be pressurised into doing illegal things by a friend, or a group of people online, or they might change their behaviour and beliefs.

This could happen if they are feeling:

- isolated and lonely or they are lacking a sense of identity or belonging
- unhappy about themselves and what others might think of them
- embarrassed or judged about their culture, gender, religion or race
- stressed or depressed
- fed up of being bullied or treated badly by other people or by society
- angry at other people or the government
- confused about what they are doing
- pressurised to stand up for other people who are being oppressed.

Someone who has been radicalised might believe that sexual, religious or racial violence is normal. They may be influenced or encouraged by what they see online. They might have links to extreme groups that preach hate like neo-Nazi groups or Daesh, also known as ISIS or IS.

It can be dangerous to have extreme views: it can lead to illegal activities involving hate incidents (which are criminal offences for which you could be arrested and charged). Remember that criminal convictions can affect your future.

How can the community help?

A community has a role to play in reducing the factors leading to terrorism or violent extremism.

A cohesive community is one where:

- there is a sense of belonging for all communities
- the diversity of people's backgrounds and circumstances is appreciated and positively valued
- those from different backgrounds have similar opportunities
- strong and positive relationships are being developed between people from different backgrounds and circumstances in the workplace, in schools and in neighbourhoods.

Activity 2

Work in small groups. List the benefits of living in a multicultural society. Use this list to write a speech/poem/rap which celebrates the diversity of Scotland.

Source 1 A multicultural society

Activity 3

Malala Yousafzai is a Pakistani woman who was shot by the Taliban when she was 12 years old, because she had been speaking out in support of education for girls. She survived and has since won the Nobel Peace Prize for her activism. She said the following about extremists:

'The extremists are afraid of books and pens. The power of education frightens them. They are afraid of women.'

1 Why do you think Malala says extremists are frightened by education?
2 To what extent do you agree?
3 Why?

Malala Yousafzai

Activity 4

We have dealt with some important issues in this learning opportunity. Now it's time to reflect upon what you have learned. Remember that if anything concerns you, there are people you can talk to.

There are teachers or other adults within school that will listen and give you advice, or signpost you towards help agencies, if necessary.

To report hate crime, go to:

• www.scotland.police.uk/keep-safe/advice-for-victims-of-crime/hate-crime/

• www.sariweb.org.uk

• or call the police on 101.

To report online material promoting terrorism or extremism: www.gov.uk/report-terrorism. Alternatively, call the police on 101.

If you are concerned that you are at risk of radicalisation or if you know someone who you think is becoming radicalised: Childline: 0800 1111 or www.childline.org.uk.

10.7 How can I contribute to my community?

By the end of 10.7 you will:

- have an understanding of community services and who provides them
- be able to name ways that volunteers contribute to their communities
- be able to identify ways in which you could contribute to your community.

Starter

Your local authority will have an obligation to provide a range of services. Do you know what those services are?

In Scotland, services are provided by various groups, for example, the local authority (council), the National Health Service (NHS), the police, national charities and agencies such as the Samaritans, local charities and voluntary community groups.

The Scottish Government encourages voluntary groups to provide a wide range of services in local communities. Visitors to our country often remark on our strong tradition of voluntary and community support. The case study on the next page is created from a number of Scottish village halls which have been mixed into one which we have called Langton.

Activity 1

Here are some problems that a community might face:
a A busy road with no pedestrian crossing.
b Nowhere for children to play.
c An elderly person who is cold and lonely.

Who should put these things right and why should it be up to them to do so?

Activity 2

Read the case study on page 155. Imagine that you have been given a building that comprises a main hall, several meeting rooms, a kitchen and lavatories, and grounds around the building that can be used for a variety of activities. The facility has full disabled access.

You need to run this community venue for the benefit of as many groups as possible.

1 Which groups do you already know about in your community who could use this venue?
2 Using the Case study for ideas, what range of activities would you introduce to attract other members of the community to use your venue?

Case study

Langton Village Hall Management Committee has run the village hall for over 85 years, providing local residents with a focal point for their social, educational and sporting activities. Every day some activity takes place in the hall, including a playgroup, yoga classes for all ages, a club for the elderly (but 'young at heart'), a dancing academy, a badminton club, indoor bowls, local art classes, a parent and toddlers group, several bridge classes, the local drama group and many more. The local Community Council also holds its monthly meetings in the hall.

The two biggest events that the management committee run are the Summer Fete and Fun Day, which is followed by a barbecue and dance in the hall. The key winter event is the annual lighting of the Christmas tree with a visit from Father Christmas.

Local groups pay to use the hall, and this income is largely used to pay for maintenance and upkeep. The hall is usually busy at the weekend for private functions and birthday parties for both young and old.

Since 1935 the hall has been run by volunteers who are elected at an annual general meeting. This committee is representative of all the hall users and the community. The Borders Council provides a handbook to assist the volunteers with managing all aspects of running the hall, such as finance, safety, and maintenance. The local residents believe that the hall is a fantastic local resource.

In the case study of Langton, volunteers have run the village hall as a community venue/centre for over 85 years. Think of the thousands of voluntary hours that members of the community would have had to donate to help the project. This would not be an unusual amount of hours for the many village halls or community centres/venues all over Scotland.

Here are some of the ways in which members of communities contribute their time in village halls and community centres/venues:

- accounting and running the finances
- cleaning
- cooking and serving meals
- fundraising
- gardening and maintenance of the grounds
- keeping the bookings diary
- keeping the building well maintained and safe
- liaising with the local council
- marketing what the facility offers
- painting and decorating
- running courses/classes

While you are still at school it won't necessarily be easy or appropriate to commit a lot of time to volunteering. However, many people your age do contribute to their communities in different ways.

Here are three organisations for young people which have a volunteering element:

'#iWill' is for young people under 20: www.iwill.org.uk.

Volunteer Scotland where anyone can find out opportunities for volunteering in their local area: www.volunteerscotland.net

The Duke of Edinburgh's Award (DofE) is for 14–24 year olds. Some schools will also offer you the chance to take part in this, usually from Third Year (S3): www.dofe.org.

Activity 3

Look at the list of activities that you generated in Activity 2 and the list of tasks the volunteers at Langton undertake. Answer the following questions:
1 Which class or activity could you help to teach or run?
2 Which tasks could you contribute to?
3 What qualities do you think you have to offer your community?

Activity 4

What do you do that makes a positive contribution to your community?

By the end of 10.8 you will:
- be able to identify appropriate support services for different needs
- be able to describe how these services support young people.

Starter

Samaritans is a well-known national agency that provides help and support. What sort of service do they offer? Who can use their service?

Case study

Samaritans

We don't know when you might need us. That's why we are open 24 hours a day.

The aim of the agency

Samaritans provides confidential non-judgemental emotional support, 24 hours a day for people who are experiencing feelings of distress or despair, including those which could lead to suicide. Samaritans say: 'Whatever you're going through, whether it's big or small, don't bottle it up. We are here for you if you're worried about something, feel upset or confused, or just want to talk to someone.'

The service it offers

People can contact them for support by telephone, email, letter and face to face in most of their branches. Samaritans is available to anyone in the UK and Ireland.

Samaritans is run by

It is a UK-wide charity with local branches and local volunteers in most major towns and cities.

Information on their website includes

Details about problems such as depression and how people can be helped; how to volunteer and support Samaritans; contact details for email and local services.

An example of someone who was helped by the Samaritans

'One night, around 2am, I phoned Samaritans. A young woman spoke to me but I just didn't know what to say. I couldn't talk about what was happening. So she asked me what I'd done that day and gradually I was able to tell her my story. As I was talking I began to feel a sense of relief as it all came out. When I came off the phone after an hour I was overwhelmed by a feeling of peace and was able to go straight to sleep. It helped so much that I called back the following night. I spoke to a few different volunteers over the next two weeks. It was the same story every night; I just needed to tell someone about it all. They were brilliant, absolutely brilliant. After I phoned Samaritans, I felt more able to get on with my life. After six months … I felt I could cope.'

People can get in touch with Samaritans to find out more by:

Phoning 116 123 (your local branch number will be in your local directory)

Source 1 A case study of a helping agency

When Samaritans was first set up, there were few agencies that specifically helped young people – today all that has changed. Samaritans is just one of many voluntary agencies that offer help to people when they need someone to turn to. Activity 1 will look at agencies that particularly support young people.

Activity 1

1   Look at Source 2, which shows three agencies that help young people. Your teacher will allocate you one of these agencies and ask you to work with other students in a small group. Your task will be to do research, assemble information and present a case study about one of these agencies. Each one of them could be invaluable to you or other students in the future – so this case study could provide crucial awareness of the sort of support that is available to someone who is facing a crisis or a difficult time.
    You could present your case study as a:
    • blog or magazine article
    • talk with PowerPoint illustrations
    • radio or television interview, with some members of your group as interviewers and others as members of the organisation.

    In your group, remember to plan your work by deciding roles and responsibilities for undertaking various parts of the case study (for example, research, creating the presentation slides, speakers, background music).

    Whatever your format, as in the Samaritans example in Source 1, ensure your case study includes:
    • the main aim of the agency
    • the services it offers to young people
    • who runs it (for example, a charity or a government department)
    • details of the sort of information you can get online
    • an example of someone who received help
    • details of how people can get in touch with the agency or find out more.
2   After each group's presentation you may want to offer your feedback. Try to identify:
    • at least one thing your group liked about the presentation content
    • at least one thing your group liked about the presentation style
    • one thing that your group thinks could have improved the presentation content
    • one thing that your group thinks could have improved the presentation style.

Childline	**childline** ONLINE, ON THE PHONE, ANYTIME childline.org.uk | 0800 1111
LGBT Youth Scotland	**LGBT YOUTH SCOTLAND**
Young Minds	**YOUNGMiNDS**

Source 2 Three helping agencies

Activity 2

If you could invite someone from one of these agencies to come in to school and talk to students, which agency would you invite? Why?

By the end of 10.9 you will:

- be able to describe what 'prejudice' and 'discrimination' mean
- know about different types of prejudice
- be able to use a range of strategies to challenge prejudice and discrimination assertively.

Starter

Look at the photographs in Source 1. They are what you would probably see and experience in any local town or city. They don't present a challenge to the majority of people, but they could cause problems for others. Who do you think might have difficulties and why?

Source 1 In and around town

People who have particular needs or disabilities can find that their needs are not taken into consideration when moving around town. Worse still, other people may decide they know what's best for someone else.

Prejudice means pre-judging people based on what a person thinks they know about them. For example, some older people might think that teenagers hanging around in their local shopping centre *must* be up to no good, even if they aren't.

All sorts of people may experience prejudice because others don't bother to get to know them or check if their opinion of that person is actually the truth.

Activity 1

1   What sorts of prejudice or discrimination might the following people experience from others in our society?

   a   A person with visual impairment (blind person).

   b   A person who uses a wheelchair to get around.

   c   A person who cannot read or speak English.

   d   A teenager wearing a 'hoodie'.

   e   A person who looks different from the majority of people around them because of the clothes they are wearing or the way they wear their hair.

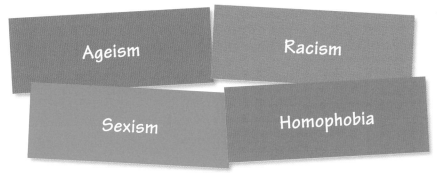

Source 2 Types of prejudice

Prejudice can lead to discrimination. This means treating somebody unfairly because of a personal characteristic. Source 2 shows some words that describe different types of prejudice.

The Equality Act 2010 protects you from discrimination:

- at work
- in education
- as a consumer
- when using public services
- when buying or renting property
- as a member or guest of a private club or association.

Under the Equality Act, there are nine protected characteristics (see Source 2 on page 139). It is against the law for anyone to discriminate against another person because of one or more of these characteristics. As we all have some of these characteristics, for example, our sex or age, we are all protected by the Act from discrimination. It's also against the law if someone tries to discriminate against you because they think you belong to a group of people who have protected characteristics.

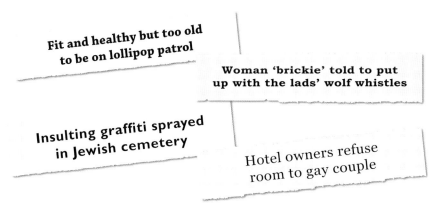

Source 3 Newspaper headlines

11 Planning for the future
11.1 What are my aspirations?

By the end of 11.1 you will:
- be able to describe what 'aspirations' are
- be able to discuss your own aspirations.

Starter

What do we mean by 'aspirations'?
In pairs, consider what you understand 'aspirations' to mean. Be prepared to feed back to the class.

'Aspirations' are what an individual would like to achieve in their life. Once you decide upon your aspirations, you can begin to take the necessary steps to achieve them.

Stuart Hogg   Laura Muir   Mhairi Black

Source 1 What do we need to achieve?

1. Who or what has been the biggest influence in your life?
2. How old were you when you started playing rugby?
3. How many hours a week do you train?
4. Do you have a special diet?
5. Are there times when you would like to give up playing rugby? If so, why?
6. Is there anything you have had to give up in order to play rugby at the level you do?
7. Is there any advice you would give to young rugby players?
8. Who or what is the most important thing in your life?
9. If you weren't a rugby player, what else would you have liked to have been?
10. Where do you see yourself in five years from now?

Source 2 Questions for Stuart Hogg, a Scottish rugby union player

Activity 1

Look at Source 1. All these people became well-known for being successful at a young age. In pairs, discuss what talents, skills, attributes and values each would have needed to achieve their success.

How important is natural talent? Is natural talent on its own enough? Are there any attributes or values that all these people would have in common?

Activity 2

Imagine you and your partner have been asked to put together a webpage on the lives of famous people to inspire young people. Prepare ten interview questions, with a focus on achieving aspirations, for one of the people in Activity 1. Source 2 gives some examples of questions you might ask.

In a study which was published in May 2017, three-quarters of young people surveyed chose becoming a YouTuber as their most desired 'job' when older. The same study also found the following statistics:

- 1 in 3 wanted to be a YouTuber (34.2%)
- 1 in 5 hoped to be a blogger or vlogger (18.1%)
- 1 in 6 aspired to be a pop or film star (16% and 15.7% respectively)
- 1 in 7 went for doctor/nurse (13.45%)
- 1 in 8 wanted to be a TV host (12.45%)
- 1 in 9 chose athlete or teacher (11.9%)
- 1 in 15 wanted to become a lawyer (6.4%)

While the study separated YouTuber, blogger and vlogger as possible future jobs, all three can be grouped as 'social media influencers'. This means that over 50 per cent of young people hope to make a living out of creating content on social media.

Source 3 Most desired career?

The survey went on to find out why these young people wanted to be YouTubers, bloggers and vloggers. It reported:

1 Creativity (24%) – today's younger generations like to be creative
2 Fame (11.4%) – being a successful YouTuber often means being more famous and influential than most traditional celebrities (like those in Activity 1)
3 Self-expression (11%) – becoming a YouTuber enables young people to express themselves
4 Money (9.8%) – not top three but still a factor
5 People (8.4%) – young people enjoy engaging and collaborating with others on social media
6 Recognition (6.1 %) – YouTubers are far more recognisable and influential than traditional celebrities (like those in Activity 1)
7 Travel (4.2 %) – being a YouTuber can involve lots of opportunity to travel.

Source 4 Aspirations

Activity 3

How do the seven points in Source 4 compare with your own aspirations? Are these the things that are important to you? What else would you like to achieve in life?

Activity 4

Reflect upon your own aspirations. What steps will you need to take to achieve these?

By the end of 11.2 you will:

- understand that people have multiple roles and responsibilities in society
- understand how different roles help make a group successful
- be able to describe why positive relationships are helpful when working in groups.

Starter

Each of us have many roles in life. Look at the picture of Ajit and the number of different roles he has in Source 1. There are probably many more that aren't even listed. Think of yourself: what roles do you have in your life?

a son

a good friend

a student

a UK citizen

a good footballer

a trumpet player

a Scout

a grandson

Source 1 This is Ajit. Ajit is …

Activity 1

This competition is to see which group can build the tallest tower.
- Each group must have exactly the same number and size of sheets of newspaper, and a roll of sticky tape.
- You are not allowed to fix your tower to any surface in the room – it must be freestanding.
- Each group is only allowed ten minutes to build their tower from newspaper and sticky tape!

What skills did you use in order to build your tower?

As you move through life you learn about what you do best and what motivates you. There is no job where you work entirely on your own. You will always be working with other people, even if it's online. So it's important to take other people's skills and attitudes into account.

Skills are things that you have learned to help you do a job well, such as good communication skills.

Attitudes are the personal characteristics and behaviours you display, such as reliability in turning up for a job.

Both are important in school and the workplace.

Activity 2

Sometimes working in a group or team isn't a happy experience. Things go wrong or the group just doesn't seem to gel.

Working in pairs, list all the reasons that get in the way of a team being happy and successful. Think about actions, words and attitudes.

Activity 3

1 What jobs, paid and unpaid, do students in your class currently do?
2 What skills and attitudes are required for each job?

Activity 4

In groups, discuss what it's like to work with other people.
1 Compare how you feel and behave when you work in:
    a large groups
    b in pairs
    c on your own.
2 What skills and attitudes are useful for **a**, **b** and **c**? Are different skills required?
3 Which skills and attitudes do members need to develop for successful group work?

Activity 5

What is your best attitude or skill that you can bring to a team?

By the end of 11.3 you will:
- understand what good listening skills are
- have practised speaking and listening to others
- be able to identify ways that good communication skills can help you work with others.

Starter

Choose a subject that you think you could talk about for 'Just a Minute'. It can be anything that interests you or you feel you know a lot about, for example, a hobby, a famous person, a sport or your favourite subject.

In pairs, talk for one minute each on your chosen topic. Try not to repeat yourself, pause too much or end up talking about something else.

Take turns and time the other person. How easy was it for each of you to talk for one minute?

Activity 1

In the Starter activity you were probably concentrating on being a good speaker – but how good a listener were you?
1 Without help from your partner:
   a Write down the three most important facts or ideas you thought you heard while *they* were speaking.
   b Write down the three most important facts or ideas that you think *you* spoke about.
   c Read your lists to each other – do they agree? Were you a good listener to what your partner was saying?

Sometimes we need to practise listening as much as speaking.
2 Work together in your pair to identify up to five things that make somebody a good listener. Then explain them to the rest of your class.

4 'Active Listening' – you are paying attention to what they say and how they say it: their feelings about the subject.
3 'Hearing the Content' – you are taking in basic facts, opinions and so on.
2 'Superficial Listening' – you are going through the motions of listening but aren't really paying attention.
1 'Ignoring' – you know the other person is talking but you are not responding to them.

Source 1 Listening skills levels

Activity 2

Work with a different person in a pair and play the 'Just a Minute' activity again.

This time, when you are the listener, choose one of the listening skills levels in Source 1 and play the role of someone listening at that level. See if your partner can guess which listening skill level you were demonstrating.

Family members

Teachers

Source 2 Talking with others

Shop assistants

One of the emergency services

Activity 3

Obviously it feels good when someone is really listening to us. In what situations is it important to be a good listener when talking with others?

Work in a small group to come up with examples where being a good listener is vital when you are communicating with the people in Source 2.

Good communication is vital for effective teamwork. In a good team, team members communicate openly with each other, sharing their thoughts, opinions and ideas with members of their team, as well as listening to and taking into consideration what others have to say. Good communication is essential for keeping track of progress and working together efficiently on tasks. Poor communication can lead to 'crossed wires' – that can mean work is left incomplete/incorrect or conflicts can arise.

Activity 4

What other skills are important when working with others?

Design a job advert. The job is not specified but the person must be a 'team player'. What skills will they need? How can they demonstrate those skills? Why are these skills important?

By the end of 11.4 you will:

- be thinking about the positive things you want in the future
- have created steps to help you achieve your goals
- know how to turn steps into targets.

Activity 1

Ellie (Source 1) lives in a happy neighbourhood and knows other people in her street, joins in local activities and helps her mum serve tea at the local senior citizens' Friendship Club.

She wants to go on her school's trip to France because she enjoyed a similar trip when she was at primary school. Her parents say that the primary school trip was not that long ago and she has had family holidays since then. They tell her they only feel able to contribute 50 per cent of the cost of this trip – but if she can raise the other 50 per cent, she can go.

1 What steps can Ellie take to raise the rest of the money?
2 What can she do on her own?
3 Will she need to work with other people?
4 In what way might she need other support from adults?

Starter

Is it easier to work towards a goal that you have set for yourself, or one that has been set for you by someone else?

Source 1 Ellie

S Specific, for example, 'I will improve the presentation of my work by always putting the date and underlining titles.' Not 'I will make my work look better.'

M Measurable, for example, 'I will improve my punctuality to 100 per cent this term.' Not 'I will try to be on time.'

A Attainable, for example, 'I will attend choir club every week.' Not 'I will sing the solo in the next school concert.'

R Realistic, for example, 'I will learn 10 new words in Spanish each week.' Not 'I will learn 50 new words in Spanish each day.'

T Time-specific, for example, 'I will aim to achieve these targets by the next half-term holiday.' Not 'I will do this as soon as I can.'

Source 2 SMART targets

We sometimes break down goals into achievable steps; we call these steps 'targets'. You may have already been setting targets at school, or perhaps this idea is new to you.

The targets you set need to be achievable, not just a hope or a wish. The best way of setting a target is to think of them as SMART targets, as explained in Source 2.

Activity 2

In the Starter activity you began to look at the reasons for setting your own personal goals. This activity gives you the chance to practise setting goals by working out steps to help someone solve a problem.
- On her way to school Timea regularly sees Archie. She would like to become friends with him. They have never had a real conversation with each other but they recognise and smile at each other, and nod 'hello'.
  Timea's goal: To become friends with Archie.
- Daniel's younger brother and sister really irritate him, and he tends to lose his temper when they are around. He knows that he has said hurtful things to them and would really like to be able to control his temper.
  Daniel's goal: To control his temper when he's around his brother and sister.
- Hari is having real difficulties in one of her subjects. She wants to improve her chances to do better. Her teacher is willing to help but points out she has fallen behind with her homework schedule. Hari has several pieces of overdue homework in more than one subject and doesn't know where to start.
  Hari's goal: To improve her study skills.

Discuss solutions for these people.

Activity 3

Here are some goals written by students your age. Turn them into SMART targets. Use Source 2 to help you work out which bit of S-M-A-R-T to use for each one.
- I'll get completely up to date with my homework.
- I'll try to visit my auntie more often.
- I must improve my piano playing.
- I am going to keep my bedroom tidy all the time.
- I'll get around to my revision before the exams start.

Activity 4

How could you apply the SMART target idea to something you want to achieve in your own life?

By the end of 11.5 you will:

- be able to describe the difference between a 'job' and a 'career'
- know what careers might suit you in the future
- know how you might begin to plan a career.

Starter

Most people want to achieve things in life but get distracted from their goals. You can stay focused by coming up with your own personal motto. For example, somebody who is good at putting things off could use the motto: 'Do it now!' What personal motto would help keep you focused on your goals?

Activity 1

Is there a difference between doing a job and having a career? Look at the list in Source 1 and decide whether you think each person is doing a job or having a career.

- Actor
- Newsreader
- Newsagent
- Nurse
- Flyer/leaflet distributor
- Parent
- Pop star
- Postman/postwoman
- Professional footballer
- Shop assistant
- Soldier
- Supermarket checkout assistant
- Teacher
- Traffic warden
- Vet
- Window cleaner

Source 1 Career or job?

Sometimes students of your age tell us that when they hear the question 'What do you want to do when you grow up?' they want to say things like:

- 'Give it a rest, it's a long time before I have to start work!'
- 'I don't know.'
- 'Be an astronaut.'
- 'Not a lot.'
- 'Be famous.'
- 'I haven't really thought about it.'

Of course, you might have thought about it … but then again maybe you haven't. No one should feel under pressure to make such a big decision at this stage in life. You will change a lot as you grow up, and new sorts of jobs and careers could be available in the future that we have not even thought of now. However, thinking about your personal strengths and interests can help you start the journey.

Skating

Writing

Making things

Walking my dog

Being outdoors

Playing with friends

Source 2 What I'm good at and what I enjoy doing

Activity 2

Make a spider diagram like the one in Source 2, with you at the centre and all the things you're good at and your interests around you. Spend some quiet time seeing where your diagram takes you.

Even the most glamorous of careers will have a tedious side to them. There will always be routines that need to be followed and qualifications that need to be gained.

Activity 3

Let's think about the example of a soldier from Source 1. The recruitment adverts usually show them on active duty (hiding in forests, climbing mountains, jumping out of planes – all looking very exciting!), but Source 3 lists some of the practical things a soldier needs to learn to do.

What would be the practical tasks and routines that each of the following would have to do?
- Member of a pop band
- Someone running a pub
- Fitness instructor at a gym
- Dancer in a musical
- Surgeon
- On-board crew for an airline
- Nanny in a celebrity family
- Morning TV presenter

1   Be awake, up and ready to work at a specific time.
2   Follow set routines for preparing your uniform.
3   Tidy your living area.
4   Clean your equipment.
5   Practise drill and exercise routines.
6   Develop teamwork skills.
7   Take responsibility for specific tasks.

Source 3 Being a soldier

There is more than one pathway to any job or career. Some people choose to stay on at school after Fourth Year (S4) while others go to college, or find a job with training or a modern apprenticeship. Some people choose to go to university after Fifth or Sixth Year (S5, S6). Others may start their own businesses. If you speak to two adults who do the same job, you will probably find that they took different routes to get there. What is important is to keep your options open so that you have choices to make. You need to build on your strengths …

Activity 4

Copy and complete the following sentence:
When I leave school, I would like people to remember my strength as …

11.6 My personal brand

By the end of 11.6 you will:
- understand how we think about our abilities and how others regard our abilities
- know what is meant by 'personal brand', and have created your own.

How do you see yourself?
- 'Do it now' person
- 'Wait and see' person
- 'Think, plan and take action' person
- 'Take opportunities as they present themselves' person
- 'Head in the clouds' person

Compare notes with the person next to you.
Are they surprised by how you see yourself?

Source 1 How do you see yourself?

At some point in your life someone has probably told you off for only thinking about yourself or being selfish.

However, believing in yourself isn't a selfish or bad thing. Belief in yourself, or self-confidence, is a vital tool in life.

Activity 1

1 Think about five positive things that describe the sort of person you think you are. Now think about the points you might like to change about yourself. Copy and complete the table below.

Positive points about the way I am now	Things about myself I want to change or develop

2 How confident do you feel about changing? As a class, discuss what holds people back from being what they want to be.

'Branding' is the marketing practice of creating a name, symbol or design that identifies and differentiates a product from other products.

Source 2 Brands on the high street

Activity 2

My personal brand

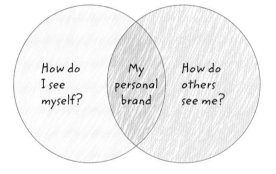

How do I see myself?

My personal brand

How do others see me?

Design a logo or symbol for your name. You might want to draft this first. Then draw your logo at the top of a sheet of paper. Now answer these questions about yourself and how others see you.

- Who are you?
- What are your values?
- What excites you?
- What good things do others say about you?
- What are you good at?
- What is your vision for the future?

Activity 3

Many companies, organisations and charities use 'branding'. Why is this? Can you identify the brands above in Source 2?

Activity 4

Share your 'My personal brand' with your partner. Is there anything you have missed?

When people apply for jobs, they write a Curriculum Vitae, often called a CV. A CV is a document which summarises an individual's unique skills, character, experience and achievements. It is never too early to start making a note of your achievements!

By the end of 11.7 you will:
- have analysed your own skills and abilities and how these will support you in your future working life
- be able to explain the importance of thinking about the future today.

Starter

At what age should you start to plan for the future?

Activity 1

Here are some tools and skills that you will need in the future. Have you already mastered them or are you still getting there? How can you show you already have these tools and skills?

Copy and complete the table below, and then compare your list with a partner.

Tool or skill	Already mastered?	Working towards?	Evidence
Sticking to deadlines			
Managing workload			
Good communication skills			
Negotiating skills			
Reliability and punctuality			
Problem-solving skills			
Flexibility			

Imagine the biggest and best luxury liner sailing across a calm sea. What do you think will happen if the mechanism for steering – the rudder – breaks? Your mind and willpower are your rudder. They steer you towards your destination.

Think about what sort of life you might like. For instance, do you want a career that allows you to:

- travel
- earn lots of money
- spend time with your family
- meet lots of interesting people
- help people
- follow a special interest?

Punctuality

Appearance

Written communication

Source 1 Getting the basics right

Now consider what would happen if you didn't give your life or career any thought at all. Without plans, most people will drift eventually. If you want to succeed at something you enjoy, you need to think and make decisions about what you want to do.

Whatever you decide to do in life, in order to get there, you need basic skills in various areas, such as those shown in Source 1. Plan to succeed by working towards developing these basic skills.

Attitude

Activity 2

1 Jake is going for an interview for a job as an estate agent. Look at the first column of the table below. How could Jake show these skills to make a good impression on the person interviewing him? Then, consider what would make the interviewer think twice before considering Jake for the job. Copy and complete the table:

Areas in which skills are required	What creates a good impression?	What creates a bad impression?
Punctuality		
Appearance (*dressing appropriately*)		
Attitude		
Written communication (*think about what would make a good impression if you are filling in a form or writing a cover letter or CV*)		
Spoken communication (*how you talk and what you say in answer to questions*)		

2 Discuss whether you think the expression 'You only have one chance to make a first impression' is true.

Spoken communication

Activity 3

The Latin expression, *carpe diem* means 'seize the day' or 'do it now'. As a class, discuss why today is a good time to start thinking about your future.

By the end of 11.8 you will:

- consider factors that may motivate your career choices
- think more widely about your future career
- be able to state a range of places to find information about careers.

Starter

1 Look at the factors in Source 1. They might influence your choice of career. Put them in order of importance – with 1 being most important and 6 least important.
2 Which factors scored most highly in your class?
3 Taken in isolation, should any of these factors alone determine your career choice?

a) Money

b) Prospects (whether you are likely to be able to progress steadily with this career, gaining more responsibility and money)

c) Satisfaction

d) Location (where the career is situated)

e) Flexibility

f) Suitability (whether you have the necessary talents and skills)

Source 1 Motivating factors

It is very important to think about your skills, interests and qualities when choosing a future career, as well as the financial rewards it might bring. This is because enjoying what you do will make your life happier.

Source 2 Chloe

Activity 1

Chloe has no idea what she wants to do when she 'grows up', but she is organised, likes researching projects and is good at maths.
1   List five different careers that might suit Chloe's talents.
2   As a class, discuss how Chloe's career choices broaden if we take into account that she loves animals and is a caring member of the class.

With so many careers open to you, it might be easy for you to decide not to think about it – after all, you have so much time.

In fact, it is not only exciting thinking about the future but it is never too early to start thinking about the opportunities open to you.

Activity 2

1   Work in pairs and come up with five possible influences on someone's career choice.
2   Now join with another pair to share and pool ideas. Rank the influences with the one considered to be the biggest influence at the top. Can you reach a consensus?
3   Did you know that TV programmes such as *One Born Every Minute* and *Call the Midwife* have caused a surge in midwifery applications? What are the issues accompanying this?

Look at information materials for midwifery starting at **www.careers. nhs.scot/careers/explore-our-careers/midwifery/**. Does it give you information on:
● qualifications needed
● training
● pay
● what the job is likely to entail
● where to get more information?

Activity 3

Choose one career that interests you most and list five ways you could find out about this job.

Activity 4

Is it important to start thinking now about what job or career you might want to have later in life? Give reasons for your answer.

By the end of 11.9 you will:
- know about the types of jobs and careers that are available to you
- understand what motivates people to work
- be able to identify what factors will motivate you.

Most people work at some time in their lives. There are various reasons for working, but for the majority of people it's because they need to earn money so that they can survive in society. Some people get extra job satisfaction because they enjoy the work that they do. Employers are keen to have people working for them who are motivated.

Starter

Why do you think it is important to be motivated by what you do? Try to think of at least five reasons.

Relationships – enjoying being with the people you work with; having self-respect.

Self-fulfilment – personal satisfaction, for example, feeling that you are doing something interesting and worthwhile.

Material comforts – the things you can buy with your salary, such as holidays, clothing, a car.

Security – a secure job where you are unlikely to be made redundant.

Status – gaining personal recognition; being in charge.

Source 1 What motivates me to work?

Activity 1

1 Look at Source 1. It's not always possible to get each of these five things from one job. If you had to put the factors in order, which one would be most important to you – and why?
2 Form your own personal priority order in the shape of the Diamond Five shown in Source 2. The top factor should be the most important to you; the bottom one should be the least important.

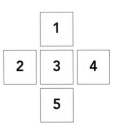

Source 2 Diamond Five

Activity 2

Now that you have thought about what motivates you to work, consider what that means for your chosen career.

Look at Source 3. Copy and complete the following table by placing each statement from Source 3 under the heading you think it fits best. Explain why you think it fits there.

Material comforts	Status	Relationships	Security	Self-fulfilment

a) To look after people	**b)** To work as part of a team	**c)** To be my own boss	**d)** To manage other people	**e)** Long summer holidays	**f)** Annual bonus payments
g) To decide how and when to do work	**h)** To stay in the same job for working life	**i)** To have good work colleagues	**j)** Not to have to take my work home with me	**k)** To be offered new opportunities	**l)** To receive recognition for my work
m) To get overtime payments	**n)** To be respected by fellow workers	**o)** To have good promotion prospects	**p)** To have good long-term prospects	**q)** To travel and stay in the best hotels	**r)** To do interesting work
s) To receive on-the-job training	**t)** To have a high level of responsibility	**u)** To get a new company car each year	**v)** To deal directly with customers	**w)** To receive good wages	**x)** To be able to see the results of my work

Source 3 What do I want from my job?

Activity 3

1 Look at the table headings from Activity 2. Choose the heading that represents the most important motivation you identified in your Diamond Five.
2 Now look at the statements that you placed underneath that heading and try to think of any jobs or careers that will give you the motivation and job satisfaction you are looking for.

Activity 4

Look at Source 4. Now write down a specific next step for yourself that fits one of the SMART target criteria, that will help you on your way to your future career.

S **Specific** (e.g. I will base my options choices on subjects I enjoy and can achieve in)
M **Measurable** (e.g. I will be on time each day this term)
A **Attainable** (e.g. I will finish projects by their deadline)
R **Realistic** (e.g. I will research which qualifications I need for my career path)
T **Time specific** (e.g. I will achieve these targets by the date I have to choose my options)

Source 4 SMART targets

By the end of 11.10 you will:
- know about some of the jobs which teenagers can do
- be able to state some of the rules regarding teenagers and work.

Starter
Look at Source 1. What are some of the typical jobs a teenager could do? Name one important skill and one important quality needed for each job.

In Scotland, the rules about employing children are set by local authorities and this means that they can differ for young people across Scotland.

The law says that, in general, children under 13 cannot be employed although they may take part in modelling, television performances, films, theatre productions, or other entertainment, advertising, and sport, but only if a child performance licence has been granted by the local authority.

If you are between 13 and 14, your local authority will have a list of jobs that you are, or are not, allowed to do.

Many students want to work to help the family finances, but it is important that they do not do so much paid work that it harms their progress in school. In Scotland there are strict rules about the hours that can be worked. There are exceptions for child actors, models and performers. Children working in these areas will need a performance licence and a chaperone. Before applying for work you should check with your local authority for the regulations that are in place there.

From 13 you can be:
- Occasionally employed by your parents doing light gardening or farming work.
- Employed by other people doing **light** work **allowed by your local authority** (e.g. a paper round).

From 14 you can:
- Work for no more than two hours on a school day and more than 12 hours in a week (not before 7 a.m. and not after 7 p.m.).
- Get a job on a Saturday for up to five hours (two on Sundays).
- Work on weekdays and Saturdays in the school holidays for five hours, with a weekly limit of 25 hours. You must not work for more than four hours without a one-hour break. During the school holidays you must be allowed two work-free weeks.

From 15 you can:
- Work up to eight hours per day, and 35 hours per week, **during school holidays**.

From 16 you can:
- Get a full-time job.
- Work as a waitress or waiter in a hotel or restaurant.

From 18 you can:
- Serve drinks from a bar.
- Become licensed to serve alcohol.

Source 2 Teenagers working in Scotland: the rules

Source 1 Typical jobs for teenagers.

Activity 1
Look at Source 2 and discuss the following questions:
1. Why were these laws made?
2. If you were to make any changes to them, what changes would you make and why?
3. Do you think a teenager working for their own family's business should have to follow these laws?

Case studies

Ropa has always done well at school and her parents have very high expectations of her. They really want her to be the first person in their family to go to university. Ropa studies hard but her grades are low in some subjects. Her parents decide to send her for extra tuition. Ropa isn't enjoying this: the tutor makes her feel stupid, she isn't sleeping well because of how worried she is and she has started feeling really bad about herself.

Patrick has a busy life. He socialises with his friends, works hard at school and has a part-time job to save up for the future. He is, however, getting exhausted. Patrick's boss wants him to work more shifts when there are big sales and more customers in the shop. Patrick would love the extra money but his exams are coming up soon.

(Photos posed by models)

Source 3 Two case studies

Children are not allowed to work:
- ✗ without an employment permit issued by the local authority, if this is required by local bylaws
- ✗ in places like a factory or industrial site
- ✗ during school hours
- ✗ before 7am or after 7pm
- ✗ for more than one hour before school (unless local bylaws allow it)
- ✗ for more than 4 hours without taking a break of at least 1 hour
- ✗ in most jobs in pubs and betting shops and those prohibited in local bylaws
- ✗ in any work that may be harmful to their health, well-being or education
- ✗ without having a 2-week break from any work during the school holidays in each calendar year

Source: based on www.gov.uk/child-employment/restrictions-on-child-employment

Source 4 Young people and employment

Activity 2

Look at Source 3 and answer the following questions:
1 What advice would you offer to Ropa to help her feel less pressurised?
2 If Patrick asked you how he should prioritise his choices, what would you say?
3 Do you agree that teenagers are under increasing pressure to achieve more in their studies and exam grades? Give reasons for your answers.

Activity 3

Look at Source 4. Young people were not consulted when these rules and regulations were brought in.
1 Do these rules and regulations do enough to protect a young person's health and safety in the workplace?
2 If you could remove something from the list, what would it be and why?
3 If you could make a new rule for the list, what would it be and why?

Activity 4

Think back over the learning opportunity and identify one important new fact about youth employment that you've learned.

By the end of 12.1 you will:
- understand that managing your money can help you save
- be able to set up a budget to cope with the unexpected.

Starter

Some people say about money, 'Easy come, easy go'. Is that really true? If you are not yet old enough to have a paid job, where does your money come from? And when you've got it, what do you use it for?

A spend, spend, spend person

A save, save, save person

A spend some, save some person

Source 1

Activity 1

People have very different attitudes to what they do with their money.

In Source 1 there are three types of people. In pairs, brainstorm the advantages and disadvantages of being each kind of person.

Activity 2

1 Imagine that you take a balanced approach to money and want to save some of it. Where do you think the best place is to save your money, and why?
- In a piggy bank
- In an ordinary account (often called a 'current account')
- In a savings account
- In a stocks and shares portfolio
2 After one year, if you don't take any money out, what do you think will have happened to your money?

Activity 3

In Activity 2 you were thinking about a balanced approach involving savings. How can we balance our approach when it comes to spending? One way is to think about our priorities.

In Source 2 there are ten things that you might spend your money on. In pairs, rank them in order of priority. Remember that you will have a limited amount to spend, so you will have to make some choices.

- ✓ Birthday present for Mum or Dad
- ✓ Pizza and cinema with friends
- ✓ Donation to a charity collection box
- ✓ Latest fashion item of clothing
- ✓ Lend money to a friend who needs it
- ✓ New music download
- ✓ Snacks
- ✓ Add data/credit to mobile phone/tablet
- ✓ Latest computer game
- ✓ Make up/toiletries

Source 2

Activity 4

Look at Table 1. Sam is trying to work out how he can afford to go away on a camping trip. At present he spends all his income each week. He needs to save a total of £30 in the next ten weeks.
1 How much does he need to save per week?
2 How can Sam make savings on his weekly spending?
3 How can Sam increase his income?
4 Copy and complete Table 1, filling in the figures for him.
5 Discuss your solutions with the class.

Current weekly income	£	Current weekly spending	£
Pocket money	5	Snacks	4
Money for chores	5	Subs	2
		Bus fares at weekend	4
TOTAL	10	TOTAL	10
New weekly income		**New weekly spending**	
		Weekly savings target	
TOTAL		TOTAL	

Table 1

Original budget

Income	£	Spending	£
Sam	30	Petrol money to and from campsite	30
Friend 1	30	Campsite fees	20
Friend 2	30	Food, etc. at £10 each	40
Friend 3	30	Entry money – local attraction at £6 each	24
		Ice creams at £1.50 each	6
TOTAL	120	TOTAL	120

Table 2 Sam's and his friends' budget for equally sharing the trip costs

Income	£	Spending	£
Sam	30	Petrol money to and from campsite	30
Friend 1	30	Campsite fees	20
Friend 2	30	Food, etc.	
		Entry money – local attraction at £6 each	
		Ice creams at £1.50 each	
TOTAL	90	TOTAL	

Table 3 Revised budget

Activity 5

Look at Table 2, which shows how Sam and his three friends budget to go on a trip.

Suddenly one friend drops out. Table 3 shows how this affects their finances. The petrol money and the campsite fees are 'fixed costs' that can't be reduced, even if there are fewer people.
1 Work out the rest of the budget.
2 What effect does one person dropping out have on their budget?
3 What changes to the budget can you suggest to make it balance?

By the end of 12.2 you will:

- be able to identify some of the reasons why we spend money
- be able to explain why we choose to support different kinds of shops
- understand how price and competition affect our consumer decisions
- understand how our consumer decisions affect other people.

Starter

Why do we spend money? In pairs, list all the things you've bought over the last month. Then discuss how much you needed the things, and whether they were luxury or impulse purchases.

The Starter activity should have got you thinking about what people of your age spend their money on and why. You are consumers and have choices about what you buy and where you buy things. You make decisions that have an impact on the economy.

Activity 1

1 As a class, brainstorm all the different types of shops you can think of.
2 Now think about how you decide where to shop. Imagine you are a typical customer at each of the shops shown in Source 1. In pairs, list all the reasons why you'd choose to shop at each, then give feedback to the class.

Source 1 Different shops

Your decision on where to spend your money doesn't just affect that particular shop. It also affects all the suppliers who provide goods and services to that shop, and it affects the other shops that you choose not to use. The different effects are shown in Source 2.

Shops	Small independent grocery shop	Large out-of-town supermarket	Designer boutique	Local speciality shop	Charity shop
Suppliers	Medium and mass market suppliers	Mass market suppliers from across UK and abroad	Design industry (clothing and goods)	Individual or small-scale suppliers from locality	People donating goods
		Advertising industry	Advertising industry	Local advertising	
		Packaging industry	Packaging industry		
		Finance industry	Finance industry		

Source 2 The different effects of choosing where to spend your money

Activity 2

Look at Source 2 and answer the following questions:
1   What would happen if consumers could get all they needed at the supermarket, and stopped using the small independent grocery shop and local speciality shops?
2   If everyone started to buy at the charity shop and no one went to the designer boutique, what might be the effects?

Activity 3

1   In Activity 1, you looked at what factors affect our decisions on where to shop. As a class, discuss whether price is the most important of those factors.
2   If price is important, imagine what would happen if one supermarket chain slashed its prices for milk. In pairs, work out a possible chain reaction in answer to these questions:
   a   Would people buy more milk there?
   b   What would happen to milk sales at other supermarkets and at the small grocery shop?
   c   Would these other shops put their prices down, too? If not, how could they compete?
   d   What impact would this have on the dairy farmers who supply the supermarket?
   e   Would the consumer pay more for local milk?
   f   What might make milk prices go back up again?
3   When shops compete with each other over price, there are winners and losers. As a class, name all the possible winners and losers, giving an explanation for each one.

Activity 4

On your own, list three things that you have learnt that a shop can do to persuade you to buy its goods rather than those from another shop.

By the end of 12.3 you will:

- have worked with others to practise the skills of creating a new business
- be able to identify ideas and methods to promote new business ideas
- have used the skills of problem-solving and action-planning.

Dragons' Den

Some of you may have watched the TV programme *Dragons' Den*. You may not know that it was first launched on television in Japan. *Dragons' Den* is now an international brand with versions airing in countries across the globe. In the programme, members of the public with ideas for new business ventures pitch for investment in the Den from the Dragons. These members of the public are enterprising people: that means they have used their creativity to develop new business ideas. The Dragons are business people who are willing to invest their own money in exchange for a share of the new business.

Starter

Look at Source 1. It shows enterprising and successful people who pitched in *Dragons' Den* with two very different products.

Have you ever wanted to invent anything?

Work with a partner to share your ideas.

Name: Amy Wordsworth
Pitching: Good Bubble
Investment required: £60 000
Investment secured: £60 000 for 40% of the company
Brief description: Children's skincare

Name: Levi Roots
Pitching: Reggae Reggae Sauce
Investment required: £50 000 for 20% of the company
Investment secured: £50 000 for 40% of the company
Brief description: Hot spicy barbecue sauce and seasonings

Source 1 Two enterprising and successful people who pitched in *Dragons' Den*

Business ideas

Finding innovative and successful new products and services isn't easy. A good way to get started is to decide on your target group and then identify the services and products they might wish to buy.

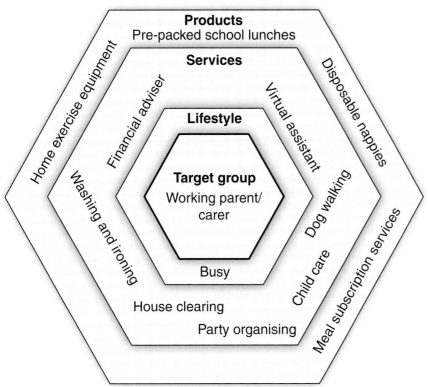

Source 2 Business ideas

BUSINESS PLAN

Business name:
What will your business be called?
Business idea:
What is the product or service?
What is its potential to be successful?
What competition will there be from others?
What risks are there and how can you limit them?
How will the product/service be promoted?
What will you charge?
Target market:
Whom is the product/service aimed at?
Why are these customers likely to buy it?
Finance:
What will you need money for?
Where might you get this money?

Source 3 A business plan

Activity 3

Now that you have your product/service and business plan ready, you need to devise a pitch for funds to start running your business.

Prepare a pitch that lasts no more than two minutes. You can use a variety of media to do this.

Finally, present your pitch to the rest of the class.

Dragons' Den was used as a model to explore some ideas about business planning. Now you will use some ideas from *The Apprentice* – a series that sets its candidates a series of challenging tasks. One of the challenges in each series is to devise an effective advertising campaign to launch a new product or service. Groups work in teams and nominate a Project Manager who is responsible for leading the task. At the end of the task, the candidates are called to the boardroom. The team with the most successful campaign wins.

Activity 4

Working in groups, choose one of the products or services from your *Dragons' Den* ideas that you thought was worth funding. Devise an advertising plan for promoting this product/service. Use Source 4 as a guide.

Remember to choose a good name for your product or business.

1 Choose the name of your product.

2 Define the USP (unique selling point) of your product – this should be the main message of the advert.

3 Know your target audience – what style of advert will appeal to them most? For example, a younger audience might be drawn to a 'busy' advert with lots of images and different fonts.

4 Choose the images that you want to appear in your advert – will they be of the product or of something else?

5 Decide where the images and text should go.

Source 4 Planning an advert to promote your product

Activity 5

Now that you have your advertising plan, in your groups, design and prepare the advert itself. You will need to ensure that you follow the plan closely. Remember to put your USP (unique selling point) across to your audience effectively.

Check your finished advert to ensure it meets all the criteria you set out in your plan.

Activity 6

In this learning opportunity you have been thinking about marketing. You have also had the opportunity to develop your group work skills.

Look at Source 5. Read the questions carefully on your own and give each section a score.

	Successful group work qualities	How did we do? Questions to ask ourselves	Self-assessment: score out of 5 5 = excellent 1 = poor
Working together	Doing my best Helping others to do their best Not giving up	How much did team members encourage each other? Did the team give up?	
Motivation	Using good communication skills Being supportive of each other all the time Using lots of different skills	Did we listen to each other? Did we discuss how to share the tasks? Did we remain supportive throughout?	
Thinking	Being creative Trying new ideas	Did we discuss various answers and solutions? Did we offer any new ideas?	
Completing the task	Seeing it through to the end Keeping focused on the task Everyone participating	Did we complete the task on time? Did we complete the task successfully? Did everyone contribute?	

Source 5 A self-assessment chart

Activity 7

Consider the pitches that were made in your version of *Dragons' Den* and the marketing you did as part of *The Apprentice* task on page 184.

Take a vote as a whole class: which idea was most worth funding and why?

Index

A

abortion 40

abuse 29, 30–1, 75, 150

additives 88

adoption 40

AIDS/HIV 46–7

alcohol 54, 56–7, 61, 76, 98
  law and 55
  mental health and 61, 76

antibiotics 84, 95

anxiety 74, 79, 81

artificial insemination 41

aspirations 160–1

assertive and aggressive speaking 24

assertiveness 24–5, 102–3

attitudes 163

B

bereavement 78–9

body image 76

budgeting 180–1

bullying 104–5

business
  ideas 185–6
  plans 185

C

cardiac arrest 97, 115, 116

careers/jobs 160, 168–9, 172–7

child sexual exploitation (CSE) 31

Childline 75, 82, 118, 153

chlamydia 44, 45

civil partnerships 26, 27, 28

commitment 26–9

common law husband and wife 27

communication skills 22–5, 102–3, 164, 165

communities 138–59

condoms 42

confidentiality 37, 96

consent, sexual 36–7

contraception 42–3

controlled drugs 49

CPR (cardiopulmonary resuscitation) 115–16

criminal convictions 151

cyberbullying 105

D

defibrillators 97

dependency, drugs and 61

depressants 50

depression 71, 80–81

diet 86–9

'difference' 140–1

discrimination 130, 139, 159

Dragon's Den 184

drugs 48–65, 76

Duke of Edinburgh's Award 91

E

e-cigarettes 59

ectopic pregnancies 39

emergency health treatment 96, 114–17

emotional wellbeing 66, 70–1, 75–7

employment law 178–9

enterprise 184–7

Equality Act 2010 129, 159

exercise 90–1

F

faith 130–1

families 122–3
  contributing to 124–5
  relationships 75–6

feelings/emotions 14–15
  managing 72–4

female bodies 8

female genital mutilation (FGM) 10–13

fertility
  and lifestyle 39
  treatment 40–1

first aid 96, 114–17

First Year (S1) 6–7

flight, fright or freeze 73

food
  symbols 88–9
  traffic light system 87

forced marriages 29

Text and photo credits

Text credits

p.5 A Charter for Young People. Protecting Children and Young People: The Charter (Scottish Executive), Crown copyright. Contains public sector information licensed under the Open Government Licence v3.0; **p.31** *t* 'Personal safety: your rights', adapted from http://www.brook.org.uk/index.php/sex-relationships/harmful-situations/abuse, *c*. From Child sexual exploitation, © NSPCC. https://www.nspcc.org.uk/preventing-abuse/child-abuse-and-neglect/child-sexual-exploitations; **p.47** Real stories explore what it's like to live with HIV through the eyes of those affected, © National Aids Trust; **p.75** Extract from 'It's All Relative' by Patrick Tolan; **p.91** Reprinted from Global recommendations on Physical activity for health, WHO. Recommendations for children and young people aged 5–17, © World Health Organization 2011; **p.95** From 'US teenager secretly gets vaccinated and attacks "conspiracy theory-believing" anti-vax parents' by Andrew Buncombe, The Independent, 12 February 2019. https://www.independent.co.uk/news/world/americas/ethan-lindenberger-vaccination-parents-controversy-measles-antivaccination-andrew-wakefield-a8774656.html. Reprinted with permission; **p.106** Data from 'Young People and gambling 2018' by The Gambling Commission **p.109** From 'You can be ex-gang but you can never be an ex murderer: Tough USA-style scheme helps youth quit' by Tom Parry. https://www.mirror.co.uk/news/real-life-stories/you-can-ex-gang-you-2081507. Used with the permission of Reach Publishing Services Limited formerly Trinity Mirror Publishing Limited; **p.109** From 'London's gangs have changed, and it's driving a surge in pitiless violence' by Andrew Whittaker and James Densley, 15 Jan 2019. https://www.theguardian.com/commentisfree/2019/jan/10/london-gangs-changed-violence-waltham-forest-drugs. Used with permission from The Guardian News & Media Limited; **pp.110, 113** Extracts from *Desert Flower* by Waris Dirie, published by Virago (an Hachette UK company), 2001. Reprinted with permission; **p.112** From 'Mother of three-year-old is first person convicted of FGM in UK' by Hannah Summers and Rebecca Ratcliffe, 1 February 2019. https://www.theguardian.com/society/2019/feb/01/fgm-mother-of-three-year-old-first-person-convicted-in-uk?CMP=share_btn_link. Reproduced with permission from PA Media; **p.115–6** '7 CPR Steps Everyone Should Know' by the Editors of Reader's Digest, originally published in Readers Digest Quintessential Guide to handling Emergencies © 2015 by Trusted Media Brands. Inc. Used by permission. All rights reserved; **p.118** From the Childline website, www.childline.org.uk © NSPCC; **p.146–7** From Universal Declaration of Human Rights, © 1948 United Nations. Reprinted with the permission of the United Nations; **p.156** from Samaritans, A case study of a helping agency, summarised from http://www.divorceaid.co.uk/emotional/help/samaritans.htm.

Photo credits